Neuropsychiatric Correlates of Alcoholism

Neuropsychiatric Correlates of Alcoholism

Edited by
IGOR GRANT, M.D.

Professor and Vice Chairman,
Department of Psychiatry,
University of California, San Diego, School of Medicine;
Assistant Chief of Psychiatry,
San Diego Veterans Administration Medical Center

AMERICAN PSYCHIATRIC PRESS, INC.
Washington, D.C.

Copyright © 1986 American Psychiatric Press, Inc.

All Rights Reserved

Manufactured in the U.S.A.

The paper used in this publication meets the minimum requirements of American National Standard for Information Sciences—Permanence of Paper for Printed Library Materials, ANSI Z39.48-1984.   ∞™

Library of Congress Cataloging in Publication Data

Main entry under title:

Neuropsychiatric correlates of alcoholism.

   (Clinical insights)
   Includes bibliographies.
   1. Alcoholism. 2. Brain—Effect of drugs on.
3. Brain—Diseases—Complications and sequelae. 4. Neuropsychiatry. I. Grant, Igor, 1942-   . II. Series. [DNLM: 1. Alcoholism. 2. Neuropsychology. WM 274 N494]
RC565.N38   1986   616.86′1   86-10760
ISBN   0-88048-127-7 (soft: alk. paper)

Contents

Contributors

KENNETH M. ADAMS, PH.D.
Chief Psychologist, Senior Medical Staff, and Division Head,
Division of Neuropsychology, Department of Psychiatry,
Henry Ford Hospital, Detroit, Michigan

NELSON BUTTERS, PH.D.
Professor of Psychiatry, University of California, San Diego,
School of Medicine, La Jolla, California; Chief, Psychology Service,
Veterans Administration Medical Center, San Diego, California

DENNIS M. DONOVAN, PH.D.
Chief, Inpatient Services, Alcohol and Drug Dependence Treatment Program,
Seattle Veterans Administration Medical Center, Seattle, Washington;
Associate Professor, Department of Psychiatry and Behavioral Sciences,
University of Washington School of Medicine, Seattle

DONALD W. GOODWIN, M.D.
Professor and Chairman, Department of Psychiatry,
University of Kansas Medical Center, Kansas City, Kansas

IGOR GRANT, M.D.
Professor and Vice Chairman, Department of Psychiatry, University of
California, San Diego, School of Medicine, La Jolla, California; Assistant Chief
of Psychiatry, Veterans Administration Medical Center, San Diego, California

MICHAEL IRWIN, M.D.
Assistant Professor of Psychiatry, University of California, San Diego, School
of Medicine, La Jolla, California; Associate Director, Alcohol Research Center,
Veterans Administration Medical Center, San Diego, California

TERRY L. JERNIGAN, PH.D.
Assistant Professor of Psychiatry and Radiology, University of California,
San Diego, School of Medicine, La Jolla, California; Staff Psychologist, Veterans
Administration Medical Center, San Diego, California

DANIEL R. KIVLAHAN, PH.D.

Chief, Outpatient Services, Alcohol and Drug Dependence Treatment Program, Veterans Administration Medical Center, Seattle, Washington; Assistant Professor, Department of Psychiatry and Behavioral Sciences, University of Washington School of Medicine, Seattle, Washington

ADOLF PFEFFERBAUM, M.D.

Associate Professor of Psychiatry and Behavioral Sciences, Stanford University School of Medicine, Stanford, California; Assistant Chief, Psychiatry Service, Veterans Administration Medical Center, Palo Alto, California

ROBERT REED, M.S.

Research Service, Veterans Administration Medical Center, San Diego, California

DOUGLAS K. ROSZELL, M.D.

Associate Chief, Alcohol and Drug Dependence Treatment Program, Veterans Administration Medical Center, Seattle, Washington; Associate Professor, Department of Psychiatry and Behavioral Sciences, University of Washington School of Medicine, Seattle, Washington

DAVID P. SALMON, PH.D.

Postgraduate Research Neuroscientist, Veterans Administration Medical Center, San Diego, California; University of California, San Diego, School of Medicine, La Jolla, California

MARC A. SCHUCKIT, M.D.

Professor of Psychiatry, University of California, San Diego, School of Medicine, La Jolla, California; Director, Alcohol Research Center, Veterans Administration Medical Center, San Diego, California

R. DALE WALKER, M.D.

Chief, Alcohol and Drug Dependence Treatment Program, Veterans Administration Medical Center, Seattle, Washington; Associate Professor, Department of Psychiatry and Behavioral Sciences, University of Washington School of Medicine, Seattle, Washington

LESLIE M. ZATZ, M.D.

Professor of Radiology, Stanford University School of Medicine, Stanford, California; Chief, Radiology Service, Veterans Administration Medical Center, Palo Alto, California

Introduction

Although the debilitating effects of immoderate alcohol consumption have been appreciated since antiquity, it is only in the past 100 years that systematic neuropathologic studies have been undertaken and only in the past 25 years that detailed neurobehavioral observations have been made. In some ways, then, the study of alcohol–brain relationships is still very new. In this monograph, some emerging data and ideas on the relationships among excessive alcohol consumption, brain structure, and behavior are reviewed.

Until fairly recently, it was common belief that alcohol abuse was the cause of any brain damage or neuropsychological deficit manifested among alcoholics. This might be true in some instances, but there is another plausible direction of causality that has received little attention until lately. Is it possible that persons with neuropsychological deficits or "minimal brain dysfunction" are actually predisposed to alcohol excess or at least might be particularly vulnerable to whatever neurotoxic effects ethanol can produce? In the first chapter in this monograph, Drs. Michael Irwin and Marc Schuckit examine the notion that persons with

Development of this monograph was made possible in part by award SA 325 from the Medical Research Service of the Veterans Administration.

family histories of alcoholism might be characterized by neurobiological "traits" that help explain the evolution of alcoholism in such persons and perhaps their vulnerability to later brain damage and neuropsychological deficits. Drs. Irwin and Schuckit show that sons of alcoholics who are themselves not alcoholic can differ from sons of nonalcoholics in a number of respects. For example, sons of alcoholics may experience less of a subjective "high" from a test dose of ethanol. The neurobiological effects of test dose may also be different: Sons of alcoholics seem to experience less body sway following ethanol intake then do controls. There may also be metabolic differences. For example, a test dose of ethanol can produce a higher accumulation of acetaldehyde in men with a family history of alcoholism compared with men who have no family history of alcoholism. Although the implications are not clear, it seems possible that if the alcohol dehydrogenase system is less active in family history positive persons, then accumulation of acetaldehyde (a by-product of alcohol degradation by the liver) can attenuate the subjective "high" and be itself neurotoxic.

Drs. Irwin and Schuckit review a number of other studies emerging from the at-risk methodology, including neurophysiological research, and the possible association of attention deficit disorder and minimal brain dysfunction to positive family history.

In the second chapter, Drs. Terry Jernigan, Adolf Pfefferbaum, and Leslie Zatz review the status of neuroradiological research in alcoholism. They note that many alcoholics are found by computed tomography (CT) to have brain shrinkage. They also note the methodological difficulties in interpreting such associations (for example, the confounding influences of age and increased variability in measurement scores). Having described a methodology to achieve statistical control over these potential sources of confounding, Dr. Jernigan and her colleagues present the results of some of their own research, which indicates that changes in sulcal and ventricular width do not occur in parallel. Specifically, these authors found that whereas alcoholics of all ages differed from controls in measures of "cortical atrophy," ventricular dilatation was observed only in older alcoholics. Such observations suggest that different mechanisms may underlie these CT abnormalities.

For example, a measure of alcohol consumption was related to cortical atrophy, whereas change in body weight was associated with ventricular dilatation. Such data suggest the possibility that sulcal measures reflect brain changes associated directly with ethanol consumption, whereas the ventricular measure might be a reflection of malnutrition.

In Chapter 3, Dr. Kenneth Adams and Robert Reed and I discuss structural and functional deficits associated with alcoholism. Many alcoholics, in the first months of abstinence, show distinctive changes in abstraction, perceptual motor skills, and memory, as well as CT scan changes. Whereas these characteristics of recently detoxified alcoholics are reasonably well agreed upon, we present some intriguing findings from research on long-term abstinence. Whereas it used to be believed that whatever functional and structural recovery was to occur was complete by the end of one month of detoxification, our new evidence suggests that this may not be the case. For example, alcoholics appear to show continuing neuropsychological recovery well into the first year of abstinence and perhaps even through the first several years of sobriety. We also note that several studies have found some reversibility in CT-measured brain shrinkage and that preliminary data from animals subjected to chronic ethanol treatment indicate considerable dendritic regrowth after prolonged "detoxification." It is our conclusion that two syndromes, commonly recognized by clinicians but absent from the *Diagnostic and Statistical Manual of Mental Disorders (Third Edition)* (American Psychiatric Association 1980) need to be considered in future research and clinical work. These include the intermediate-duration organic mental disorder associated with alcoholism and subacute dementia associated with alcoholism.

From a historical standpoint, the neuropathological change that was first clearly associated with alcoholism was punctate hemorrhages in the periventricular and periaqueductal gray. These findings were reported in 1888 by Wernicke in his study of three patients, two of them alcoholic, with rapidly progressive ophthalamoplegia and delirium. In Chapter 4 of this monograph, Drs. Nelson Butters and David Salmon describe recent progress in understanding the neurobehavioral and neuropathologic underpinnings of the Wernicke-Korsakoff syndrome. They point out that the amnesia of the Korsakoff patient is similar to that of the Alzheimer's patient, yet certain other cognitive features of DAT can help distinguish between it and the Wernicke-Korsakoff syndrome. Other dementing disorders with memory loss (for example, Huntington's disease) can be distinguished from the Wernicke-Korsakoff syndrome on the basis that the Huntington's disease patient apparently has difficulties in initiating certain kinds of retrieval that may not be evident in the Wernicke-Korsakoff patient. Drs. Butters and Salmon also review the overlaps and divergences between non-Korsakoff and Korsakoff types of alcoholic brain disease. Although chronic exposure to ethanol might explain many findings of ordinary alcoholic brain disease, it is evident that some other acute factor, most probably nutritional, triggers the Korsakoff process. On the neuropathologic level, Drs. Butters and Salmon review behavioral and neuropathological evidence that suggests the Wernicke-Korsakoff syndrome, commonly thought to be a "diencephalic" encepalopathy, probably also includes a "basal forebrain" component.

Next, in Chapter 5, Drs. Dale Walker, Dennis Donovan, Daniel Kivlahan, and Douglas Roszell shift the focus from description and speculation about causality to predictive influence of neuropsychological deficit on outcome of alcoholism treatment. They present data showing that alcoholics who have normal neuropsychological abilities during their inpatient treatment phase are more likely after six to nine months to stay abstinent and regain employment. Although duration of treatment (that is, two weeks versus seven weeks) did not seem to influence outcome in these neuropsychologically unimpaired alcoholics, those who were impaired appeared to fare better after the longer treatment duration.

In the second section of their chapter, Dr. Walker and his colleagues present a clustering approach to developing neuropsychological subgroups of alcoholics that might have implications for treatment outcome. Once again, alcoholics who had severe neuropsychological impairment were much less likely to remain abstinent during a nine-month follow-up than were those who had mild or no impairment. In another interesting clustering approach, these authors attempted to use data from several domains—neuropsychology, demographics, drinking practices, the Minnesota Multiphasic Personality Inventory (MMPI)—to develop a more complete picture of possibly homogeneous subgroups of alcoholics.

In the final chapter of this monograph, Dr. Donald Goodwin identifies four problem areas (or puzzling questions) that have emerged from recent research on alcohol and the brain. These include the need to explain divergent neuropsychological and neuroradiological results; the importance of emerging data on reversibility; the possibility that neurobiology can "cause" alcoholic drinking, rather than drinking "causing" neurobiological disturbance; and the likelihood that there may be distinct subtypes of alcoholics separable on the basis of biology and behavior. Dr. Goodwin's reprise underscores the complexity of the alcohol-brain relationship and the need for prospective studies both on at-risk offspring and alcoholics themselves who have had the benefit of very long-term periods of abstinence.

I would like to express my deep appreciation to Robert Reed, Megan Cunningham, Debi Taylor, and Anne Larsen for their assistance in preparing this monograph.

Igor Grant, M.D.

1

Neurophysiologic and Psychologic Characteristics of Men at Risk for Alcoholism

Michael Irwin, M.D.
Marc A. Schuckit, M.D.

1

Neurophysiologic and Psychologic Characteristics of Men at Risk for Alcoholism

The work presented in this monograph focuses primarily on the chronic effects of alcohol abuse on neuropsychologic processes. The researchers have either compared neuropsychologic findings in alcoholic patients and controls or followed cognitive changes in these patients over time. This chapter adds another level of thought to these studies of nervous tissue functioning of the alcoholic. Although there are definite effects of alcohol on the brain, some of the neurophysiologic and psychologic deficits found in the alcoholic patient may not be the direct consequence of alcohol. Rather, they may have been present before the chronic use of alcohol and may have contributed to the individual's vulnerability to the effects of this substance (1).

First in this chapter, data are reviewed that indicate that the development of alcoholism is a genetically influenced vulnerability. Then possibly clinically important differences between men at high future alcoholism risk and normal men are reviewed; neurophysiologic and psychologic characteristics that might be present before the onset of the illness are emphasized.

This work was supported by the Veterans Administration Research Service, National Institute of Alcohol Abuse and Alcoholism Grant 05526-03, and the Joan B. Kroc Foundation.

STUDIES SUPPORTING THE IMPORTANCE OF GENETIC FACTORS IN ALCOHOLISM

The role of genetic factors in the development of alcoholism has been supported by evidence from family, twin, and adoption studies (2,3). Family studies reveal that up to 66% of alcoholics have an alcoholic biological first- or second-degree relative; at least 31% have an alcoholic parent. The same is true for only 12% of "other" psychiatric patients, 7% of schizophrenics, and 5% of controls (4).

In the second approach, the concordance for alcoholism has been found to range from 55% to 80% in identical twins, whereas fraternal twin concordance usually does not exceed 30% (1,5–7). This supports a genetic factor in alcoholism: Identical twins with an identical genome are more concordant for alcoholism than fraternal twins who are no more genetically alike than any two full siblings.

Adoption-type studies also indicate the importance of genetic factors. When sons or daughters of alcoholics are adopted and raised without knowledge of their biological parents' problem, their rate of alcoholism is still four times higher than in controls (3). Neither an alcoholic rearing parent or an early parental loss appears to increase this risk (3,8). Longitudinal, prospective studies of cohorts of children have similarly demonstrated that adult alcoholism is significantly predicted by the presence of an alcoholic biological parent (12,13).

Although these findings document the importance of genetics in alcoholism, they do not prove it. First, the association between adult alcoholism and the presence of illness in the biological versus the rearing parent could reflect the effects of parental drinking on nonchromosomal material in the ejaculate or egg. Second, even though most children of alcoholics do not have the physical or intellectual characteristics resembling the fetal alcohol syndrome (14,15), the mother could have used alcohol or drugs excessively during gestation. Such use then influences the drinking patterns of the children in adulthood. Third, adults with psychiatric or behavioral problems may be likely to choose selectively ill partners from the general population (that is, they undergo assortative mating) (16,17,18). Several studies have demonstrated that alcoholic men are more likely to marry women with other psychiatric disorders and that most alcoholic women marry alcoholic men (17).

Despite some controversy about the findings of the genetic studies, extensive evidence does support the probable importance of genetic factors in alcoholism (19). On the basis of these studies, it is unlikely that the genetic factors are inherited in a sex-linked or simple Mendelian pattern. The complex expression of a vulnerability to alcoholism is best described by multiple genes interacting with environmental factors (17,19,20). There may be subtypes of alcoholism of different sensitivity to environmental events (21), and there may be more than one type of genetic vulnerability operating in different families (22).

TRAITS IN THOSE AT RISK FOR ALCOHOLISM

In the final analysis, most studies support the importance of genetic factors in alcoholism and justify a search for factors that could mediate the increased alcoholism risk. These investigations usually search for traits that are observable before the illness begins and are possibly linked to the predisposition (7). These trait markers of vulnerability differ from state markers; the latter are observed only during the illness.

Several approaches identify valid trait markers. For example, multiple members of several families can be studied in an effort to identify a trait that is observed in those individuals who develop the illness. This association or linkage of a trait with the illness would help reveal a pattern of inheritance in the family. However, this method is often not generally useful when the disorder is polygenic, and multiple trait markers might operate in different families.

Another approach is to study relatively large groups of subjects from a large number of families and compare them with controls. The assets of such an approach include the almost inexhaustible number of potential subjects, the study of a large number of different families and different factors, and the ability of the investigator to observe high-risk individuals before alcoholism develops.

In our research, we have opted to study populations at high risk for alcoholism by identifying young men who were not yet alcoholic but who have an alcoholic first-degree relative (23–42). The sons of alcoholics (family history positive, or FHP) are sampled from a population of male students and nonacademic staff members, age 21 to 25, at the University of California, San Diego. Because men can be expected to show a higher rate of expression of the vulnerability if it is present, the focus of these studies is on them (20,43). This high-risk group is then matched on demographics and drinking history with controls with no family history of alcoholism (family history negative, or FHN). Matched pairs of individuals with a positive or negative family history are then evaluated in the laboratory for differences in personality, ethanol metabolism, and the body's reactions to drinking. In the next section, the results from some high-risk studies are reviewed.

SOME RESULTS FROM STUDIES OF POPULATIONS AT HIGH RISK

Group Differences on Personality Measures

There is evidence that personality factors can be genetically influenced (44). During the immediate postwithdrawal period, alcoholics have been shown to have unique patterns on the Minnesota Multiphasic Personality Inventory (MMPI) (45) and elevated levels of anxiety (45). However, in our laboratory multiple measures of personality have revealed almost identical scores for FHPs and FHNs on the Rathus Assertiveness Schedule, the Spielberger Trait Anxiety Inventory (with a trend for higher trait anxiety for the FHN), the extroversion and neuroticism scales of the Eysenck Personality Inventory, and the Locus of Control Test (measuring whether individuals feel they are in charge of their lives or if external events control them). Although there is no evidence FHP men differ from FHN men on personality measures (26,46,47,48), interpretation of these results must consider that the subjects were Caucasian young men who attended college. Investigations of younger and more antisocial relatives of alcoholics have revealed group differences in personality measures. This trend, although interesting, may be of limited generalizability; further work in this area is required.

Possible Differences in Metabolism of Ethanol

When ethanol is given orally, family history is not related to the time to peak blood alcohol concentration (BAC), magnitude of that peak, or rate of ethanol disappearance (24,48–50). The accumulation of acetaldehyde in the blood, the first breakdown product of ethanol, might differ between FHP and FHN matched pairs (32,35,38,39,51), but these results are jeopardized by questions about the validity and sensitivity of the acetaldehyde assays (52, 53). If sons of alcoholics have higher levels of acetaldehyde after drinking, this might increase the risk for alcoholism via increased organ damage or a different type of intoxication at modest BACs. However, the relation of ethanol metabolism to the expression of alcoholism remains unclear.

Differences in the Reaction to Ethanol

A third factor that might influence the risk for alcoholism is the level of subjective feelings of intoxication following an ethanol load. An individual with impaired ability to estimate the degree of intoxication at a given BAC may be less able to moderate drinking habits (54). To test whether a less intense reaction to alcohol might relate to risk for alcoholism, a series of subjective and cognitive/psychomotor tests were administered to high- and low-risk groups to monitor the effects of 0.75 ml/kg dose of ethanol. Three studies from our laboratory have documented less intense subjective feelings of intoxication in FHP men (25,28,55). First, the subjects completed a Subjective High Assessment Scale (SHAS) at baseline and every 30 minutes after consumption of 0.75 ml/kg of ethanol (25). Intoxication, measured by the SHAS, was significantly less intense in the FHP subjects than in the FHN subjects despite identical BACs. The second study replicated this finding using a version of the SHAS modified to generate a total intoxication score (55). To control further for possible group differences in the expectations of the effects of ethanol and observe reactions to two different ethanol doses and placebo, a third study was completed (28). Again, postdrinking BACs were identical for the two family history groups, and FHPs and FHNs showed no differences in expectations of the effects of drinking; however, the FHP men experienced less intense feelings of intoxication than FHN men. This decreased intensity of subjective feelings of intoxication has also been corroborated in two laboratories (40,56).

Similar group differences on more objective measures of reaction to ethanol have also been documented. One aspect of a subject's motor performance can be measured by static ataxia or body sway. At baseline the level of body sway for the two family history groups was virtually identical. However, following the 0.75 ml/kg dose of ethanol, an increase in body sway was significantly less for the FHP group than for the FHN group (31). Measures of neuroendocrine change with ethanol also reveal group differences. Preliminary investigations have shown FHPs to have significantly less increase in blood cortisol (57) and in the anterior pituitary hormone, prolactin, following a single ethanol dose (58).

Accompanying these findings is the consistent trend for FHP subjects to show less deterioration on seven cognitive and neuropsychomotor tests after ingestion of 0.75 ml/kg of ethanol. A variety of tests were chosen to sample memory (paired associates), motor performance (Grooved Pegboard, Pursuit Rotor, and Reaction Time/Movement Time), visuoperceptual performance (Digit Symbol and Divided Attention Task), and visuoconceptual performance (Digit Symbol and Divided Attention Task) and abilities (Trail Making Test). Table 1 presents a brief overview of these from a small number of FHP/FHN pairs. This data indicate that the average performance decreased for both FHP and FHN, after controlling for the placebo effects. In no test was the amount of change after drinking greater for FHPs than FHNs, and in five of the seven tests the change was almost twice as high for FHNs.

In summary, our work indicates that populations at high risk for alcoholism appear to have a different reaction to ethanol; subjective intoxication after drinking and related physiological responses are less in FHP subjects than in FHN subjects. The group differences in reactions occur despite identical BAC and suggest that response to alcohol may be related to vulnerability, at least in this group of young white men.

Neuropsychologic Characteristics of Those at Risk

Several researchers examining other high-risk populations have sought evidence of baseline cognitive and intellectual deficits (59). For example, in one study, about 25% of 6- to 11-year-old offspring of alcoholics versus only 2% of controls were labeled mentally deficient in school performances (60). Second, children and non-alcoholic adult relatives of alcoholics have been reported to have poorer performance on verbal IQ and some educational test scores including auditory word span and reading comprehension (61). These studies of cognitive deficits have also indicated that FHP males have an increased number of errors on the Halstead Categories Test and a variety of vocabulary, memory, or psychomotor tests. A trend toward problems in constructional praxis and ab-

Table 1. Average Performance Decrement After 0.75 ml/kg Ethanol in Men With Positive and Negative Family Histories of Alcoholism

Test	Number of pairs	% of men with positive family history	% of men with negative family history
Paired associates	19	9.8	16.8
Trail making test B	15	3.0	9.7
Grooved pegboard	15	4.0	5.3
Reaction time	15	3.5	8.5
Digit symbol	15	5.3	6.0
Pursuit rotor, 60 RPM errors	15	41.1	62.4
Differential Aptitude Test, total score	14	6.5	10.5

stract problem solving has also been reported in men at risk for alcoholism (56,62–65).

These results, however, differ from those in our laboratory as well as the findings of Vaillant. For the latter, long-term follow-up of central city children revealed no correlation between IQ at the time of original study and future alcoholism. College students tested in our laboratory have shown no FHP/FHN cognitive differences in the baseline (prealcohol) state (28,31).

It is probable that these different findings reflect methodologic issues such as sample selection (for example, in some studies antisocial populations or groups in which parents had other diagnoses, such as schizophrenia, were examined). Differences can also relate to small sample sizes (for example, studies in which small groups were tested with a large number of tests), and some results may relate to the effects of childhood environmental problems (that is, trauma, childhood neglect, nutritional difficulties).

Electroencephalic Differences and the Risk for Alcoholism

Neurophysiological studies have used auditory or visual event-related potentials (ERPs) as a measure of brain function. Auditory ERPs represent computer-averaged brain waves measured by exposing subjects to a train of stimuli (for example, clicks or flashes of light) when they are asked to discriminate a randomly occurring unusual stimulus. Recognition of the anticipated unusual event is associated with a positive brain wave between 300 and 500 msec following the stimulus (the P300). Measures of the amplitude and latency of this wave are related to the importance of the task, the unpredictability of the event, and the subject's motivation (67). Ethanol administration affects this measure by increasing the latency and decreasing the amplitude of the P300.

Auditory brain potentials in chronic alcoholics reveal possibly permanent increased neural transmission time (that is, increased latency) as well as lower P300 amplitudes than controls (67–69). The possibility of similar deficits predating the chronic use of alcohol has recently been examined in the study of FHP and FHN groups. Sons of alcoholics may demonstrate lower amplitudes for the P300 and perhaps for the negative wave at 430 ms (30,41,68, 70). Although these studied populations are relatively small, the results have potential biological importance; young men at risk for alcoholism may be either unwilling or unable to pay as much attention to their surroundings.

Several studies have also observed that even after prolonged abstinence some alcoholics may not generate the expected amount of alpha waves in the background cortical EEG (70,71). Similar findings have been reported in relatives of alcoholics, who are also more likely to have a relatively greater increase in the amount of the alpha waves after alcohol challenge (56,62,72–76). Although it is not clear if an alpha pattern is associated with relaxation or comfortable feelings, it may be that those at increased risk for alcoholism also have a greater increase in alpha waves, and thus experience greater reinforcing effects from the use of alcohol.

The Relationship of Hyperactivity and Alcoholism

Symptoms of hyperactivity during childhood and residual signs of attention deficit disorder have been retrospectively reported by many alcoholics (65,72,78,79–81). Furthermore, children who have hyperactive symptoms are also more likely to have an alcoholic biological parent than are children who do not have hyperactivity (65,82,83). These findings suggest a possibility that minimal brain dysfunction might be closely related to an alcoholism vulnerability.

The strength and clinical relevance of such an association is, however, controversial. Symptoms of hyperactivity are not limited to attention deficit disorder (ADD) and can be seen temporarily in children living in stressful situations (86). Symptoms of impulsivity and inattention found in ADD also resemble problems observed in conduct disorder or early antisocial personality disorder (ASPD). Because ASPD appears to be associated with a high risk for drinking problems and is an independent disorder from alcoholism, some of the association between childhood impulsivity and later drinking problems may have little to do with primary alcoholism (31–38). Finally, prospective longitudinal studies have not supported an association between clinically diagnosable hyperactive syndrome and the future development of alcoholism (12,13). Although further research may find that hyperactivity symptoms may possibly be associated with the development of alcoholism, many findings might be explained by the stress of being raised by an alcoholic parent or the presence of an antisocial personality disorder.

CONCLUSION

The research reviewed in this chapter highlights a number of factors that might be associated with the vulnerability to alcoholism. Although environment is important in expressing this disorder, some of the risk may be related to genetically influenced biological factors. In the final analysis, it is unlikely that any one factor will fully explain the alcoholism risk; alcoholism is probably a polygenic, multifactorial disorder.

There is much data indicating that children of alcoholics, who are themselves more likely to develop alcoholism, differ from those who have no alcoholic relative. One consistent finding has been a decreased intensity of reaction to ethanol in sons of alcoholics. Intoxication, when measured subjectively and by objective measures of ethanol-induced change in static ataxia, cognitive performance, and levels of neurohormones is less in those individuals with a family history of alcoholism. Second, the FHP group shows important neurophysiological differences from FHNs.

Despite the consistencies within our own data, much work needs to be done to establish the generalizability of these findings to other age groups and races and to women. If, however, a decreased intensity of reaction to ethanol or a dampened P300 amplitude are general markers associated with alcoholism vulnerability, establishing the biological mechanism, the extent of genetic control, and the possible linkage with actual expression of alcoholism will be important.

In summary, additional chapters in the monograph demonstrate cognitive and neuropsychologic differences between alcoholic patients and controls. Many of these differences result from the effects of alcohol on the brain. However, in interpreting data, it is important to recognize that some physiologic and psychologic deficits seen in alcoholics may have been present before the high alcohol intake or might reflect some unique vulnerabilities seen in men and women at high risk for alcoholism.

References

1. Schuckit MA: Trait (and state) markers of a predisposition to psychopathology, in Physiological Foundations of Clinical Psychiatry. Edited by Judd LL, Groves P. Philadelphia, Lipincott (in press)

2. Schuckit MA: Genetic and biochemical factors in the etiology of alcoholism, in Psychiatry Update, Vol. 3. Edited by Grinspoon L. Washington, DC, American Psychiatric Press, 1984

3. Schuckit MA, Goodwin DW, Winokur GA: A study of alcoholism in half-siblings. Am J Psychiatry 128:1132–1135, 1972

4. Cotton NS. The familial incidence of alcoholism: a review. J Stud Alcohol 40:89–116, 1979

5. Gurling HM. Genetic epidemiology in medicine—recent twin research. Br Med J 288:3–5, 1984

6. Kaij L. Studies on the etiology and sequels of abuse of alcohol. Department of Psychiatry, University of Lund, Sweden. 1960

7. Murray RM, Clifford C, Gurling HMD, et al: Current genetic and biological approaches to alcoholism. Psychiatric Development 2:179–192, 1983

8. Goodwin DW, Schulsinger F, Moller N, et al: Drinking problems in adopted and nonadopted sons of alcoholics. Arch Gen Psychiatry 31:164–169, 1974

9. Goodwin DW, Schulsinger F, Hermansen L, et al: Alcohol problems

in adoptees raised apart from alcoholic biological parents. Arch Gen Psychiatry 28:238–243, 1973

10. Cadoret RJ, Cain CA, Grove WM: Development of alcoholism in adoptees raised apart from alcoholic biologic relatives. Arch Gen Psychiatry 37:561–563, 1980

11. Bohman M, Sigvardsson S, Cloninger R: Maternal inheritance of alcohol abuse. Arch Gen Psychiatry 38:965–969, 1981

12. Vaillant GE, Milofsky ES: The etiology of alcoholism: a prospective viewpoint. Am Psychol 37:494–502, 1982

13. Vaillant GE: The course of alcoholism and lessons for treatment, in Psychiatry Update, Vol. 3. Edited by Grinspoon L. Washington, DC, American Psychiatric Press, 1984

14. Streissguth AP, Landesman-Dwyer S, Martin JC, et al: Teratogenic effects of alcohol in humans and laboratory animals. Science 209:353–361, 1980

15. Streissguth AP: Alcohol-related morbidity and mortality in offspring, in Drinking Women—Alcohol Studies. Edited by Schuckit MA. NJ, Rutgers University Press (in press)

16. Lucero JR, Jensen KF, Ramsey C: Alcoholism and teetotalism in blood relatives of abstaining alcoholics. Quarterly Journal of Studies on Alcoholism 32:183–185, 1971

17. Kaij L, Dock J: Grandsons of alcoholics: a test of sex-linked transmission of alcohol abuse. Arch Gen Psychiatry 32:1379–1381, 1975

18. Stabenau JR, Hesselbrock V: Clinical study: assortative mating, family pedigree and alcoholism. Subst Alcohol Actions Misuse 1:375–380, 1980

19. Robins LN: Sturdy childhood predictors of adult antisocial behavior: replications from longitudinal studies. Psychol Med 8:611–622, 1978

20. Shields J: Heredity and environment, in A Textbook of Human Psychology. Edited by Eysenck HJ, Wilson GD. Lancaster, England, MTP Press, 1976

21. Cloninger CR, Christiansen KO, Reich T, et al: Implications of sex differences in the prevalences of antisocial personality, alcoholism, and criminality for familial transmission. Arch Gen Psychiatry 35:941–951, 1978

22. Zubin J, Spring B: Vulnerability—a new view of schizophrenia. J Abnorm Psychol 86:103–126, 1977

23. Schuckit MA, Bernstein LI: Sleep time and drinking history: a hypothesis. Am J Psychiatry 138:528–530, 1981

24. Schuckit MA: Peak blood alcohol levels in men at high risk for the future development of alcoholism. Alcoholism: Clinical and Experimental Research 5:64–66, 1981

25. Schuckit MA: Self-rating alcohol intoxication by young men with and without family histories of alcoholism. J Stud Alcohol 41:242–249, 1980

26. Schuckit MA: Anxiety and assertiveness in the relatives of alcoholics and controls. J Clin Psychiatry 43:238–239, 1981

27. Saunders GR, Schuckit MA: MMPI scores in young men with alcoholic relatives and controls. J Nerv Ment Dis 168:456–458, 1981

28. Schuckit MA: Subjective response to alcohol in sons of alcoholics and controls. Arch Gen Psychiatry 41:879–884, 1984

29. Schuckit MA, Engstrom D, Alpert R, et al: Differences in muscle-tension response to ethanol in young men with and without family histories of alcoholism. J Stud Alcohol 42:918–924, 1981

30. Elmasian R, Neville H, Woods D, et al: Event-related brain potentials are different in individuals at high and low risk for developing alcoholism. Proc Natl Acad Sci USA 79:7900–7903, 1982

31. Schuckit MA: Ethanol-induced changes in body sway in men at high alcoholism risk. Arch Gen Psychiatry 42:375–379, 1985

32. Schuckit MA, von Wartburg JP: Acetaldehyde levels in men at high risk for future alcoholism. Presented at the annual meeting of the

International Society for Biological Research in Alcoholism, Santa Fe, NM, June 1984

33. Schuckit MA: Alcoholism and genetics: possible biological mediators. Biol Psychiatry 15:437–447, 1980

34. Schuckit MA: Biological markers: metabolism and acute reactions to alcohol in sons of alcoholics. Pharmacol Biochem Behav 13:9–16, 1980

35. Schuckit MA, Rayses V: Ethanol ingestion: differences in blood acetaldehyde concentrations in relatives of alcoholics and controls. Science 203:54–55, 1979

36. Schuckit MA: A study of young men with alcoholic close relatives. Am J Psychiatry 139:791–794, 1982

37. Lipscomb TR, Nathan PE: Blood alcohol level discrimination: the effects of family history and alcoholism, drinking pattern and tolerance. Arch Gen Psychiatry 37:571–576, 1980

38. Zeiner AR, Nichols N, Krug R: Offspring of alcoholic and social drinker parents. Alcoholism: Clinical and Experimental Research 7:127, 1983

39. Zeiner AR, Krug R, Kegg P, et al: Cardiovascular and pharmacokinetic effects of ethanol in offspring of alcoholics and social drinkers. Presented at the 20th International Congress of Applied Psychology, Edinburgh, Scotland, July 1982

40. O'Malley SS, Maisto SA: The effects of family drinking history on responses to alcohol: expectancies and reaction to intoxication. J Stud Alcohol (in press)

41. Schmidt AL, Neville JH: Event-related brain potentials (ERPs) in sons of alcoholic fathers. Presented at the annual meeting of the International Society for Biological Research in Alcoholism, Santa Fe, NM, June 1984

42. Schuckit MA, Gunderson EK, Heckman NA, et al: Family history as a predictor of alcoholism in U.S. Navy personnel. J Stud Alcohol 37:1678–1685, 1976

43. Schuckit MA, Morrisey ER: Alcoholism in women: some clinical and social perspectives with an emphasis on possible subtypes, in Alcoholism Problems in Women and Children. Edited by Greenblatt M, Schuckit MA. Grune and Stratton, 1976

44. Schuckit MA, Haglund R: Etiological theories on alcoholism, in Alcoholism. Edited by Estes N, Heinemann ME. St. Louis, Mosby, 1982

45. Tarter RE, Alterman AI: Neurobehavioral theory of alcoholism etiology, in Theories of Alcoholism. Edited by Chaudron G, Wilkinson D. Addiction Research Foundation (in press)

46. Schuckit MA: Extroversion and neuroticism in young men. Am J Psychiatry 140:1223–1224, 1983

47. Morrison C, Schuckit MA: Locus of control in young men with alcoholic relatives and controls. J Clin Psychol 44:306–307, 1983

48. Utne HE, Hensen FV, Winkler K, et al: Alcohol elimination rates in adoptees with and without alcoholic parents. J Stud Alcohol 38:1219–1223, 1977

49. Behar D, Berg CJ, Rapport JL: Behavioral and physiological effects of ethanol in high-risk and control children: a pilot study. Alcoholism 7:404–410, 1983

50. Knop J, Goodwin D, Teasdale TW, et al: A Danish prospective study of young males at high risk for alcoholism, in Longitudinal Research in Alcoholism. Edited by Goodwin DW, Teilmann Van Dusen K, Mednick SA. Boston, Kluwer-Nijhoff, 1984

51. Ward K, Weir DG, McCrodden JM, et al: Blood acetaldehyde levels in relatives of alcoholics following ethanol ingestion. International Research Communications System Med Sci 11:950, 1983

52. Lindros KO: Human blood acetaldehyde levels: with improved methods, a clearer picture emerges. Alcoholism: Clinical and Experimental Research 7:70–75, 1983

53. Eriksson CJ: Human blood acetaldehyde concentration during etha-

nol oxidation (updated 1982). Pharmacol Biochem Behav 18: 141–150, 1983

54. Nathan PE, Lisman SA: Behavioral and motivational patterns of chronic alcoholism, in Alcoholism: Interdisciplinary Approaches to an Enduring Problem. Edited by Tarter RE, Sugerman AA. Reading, MA, Addison-Wesley, 1976

55. Schuckit MA, Duby J: Subjective reaction to alcohol in sons of alcoholics and controls. Presented at the annual meeting of the Research Society on Alcoholism, New Orleans, LA, May 1982

56. Mednick SA: Subjects at risk for alcoholism: recent reports. Presented at the annual meeting of the Research Society on Alcoholism, Houston, TX, April, 1983

57. Schuckit MA: Differential effect of ethanol on plasma cortisol in relatives of alcoholics and controls: preliminary results. J Clin Psychiatry 45:374–379, 1984

58. Schuckit MA, Parker DC, Rossman LR: Ethanol-related prolactin responses and risk for alcoholism. Biol Psychiatry 18:1153–1159, 1983

59. Becker JT, Butters N, Hermann A, et al: A comparison of the effects of long-term alcohol abuse and aging on the performance of verbal and nonverbal divided attention tasks. Alcoholism: Clinical and Experimental Research 7:213–216, 1979

60. Herjanic BM, Herjanic M, Penick EC, et al: Children of alcoholics. Presented at the annual meeting of the Research Society on Alcoholism, Washington, DC, May, 1976

61. Hedegus AM, Alterman AI, Tarter RE: Learning achievement in sons of alcoholics. Alcoholism: Clinical and Experimental Research 8:330–333, 1984

62. Gabrielli WF, Mednick SA: Intellectual performance in children of alcoholics. J Nerv Ment Dis (in press)

63. Schaeffer KW, Parsons OA, Yohman JR: Neuropsychological differ-

ences between male familial and nonfamilial alcoholics and nonalcoholics. Alcoholism: Clinical and Experimental Research (in press)

64. Tarter R, Hill S, Jacob T, et al: Neuropsychological comparison of sons of alcoholic depressed and normal fathers. Presented at the annual meeting of the International Society for Biological Research in Alcoholism, Santa Fe, NM, June 1984

65. Tarter RE, Hegedus AM, Goldstein G, et al: Adolescent sons of alcoholics: neuropsychological and personality characteristics. Alcoholism: Clinical and Experimental Research 8:216–222, 1984

66. Vaillant GE, Milofsky ES: Natural history of male alcoholism. Arch Gen Psychiatry 39:127–133, 1982

67. Porjesz B, Begleiter H: Brain dysfunction and alcohol, in The Pathogenesis of Alcoholism. Edited by Kissin B, Begleiter H. New York, Plenum Press, 1983

68. Begleiter H, Porjesz B, Bihari B: Brain potentials in boys at risk for alcoholism. Presented at the annual meeting of the American Psychiatric Association, Los Angeles, May 1984

69. Begleiter H: Event-related potentials in children of alcoholics and controls. Presented at the annual meeting of the International Society for Biological Research in Alcoholism. Santa Fe, NM, June 1984

70. Propping P, Kruger J, Mark N: Genetic disposition to alcoholism. An EEG study in alcoholics and their relatives. Hum Genet 59:51–59, 1981

71. Propping P, Kruger J, Janah A: Effect of alcohol on genetically determined variants of the normal electroencephalogram. Psychiatry Res 2:85–98, 1980

72. Pollock VE, Volavka J, Mednick SA, et al: A prospective study of alcoholism: electroencephalographic finding, in Longitudinal Research in Alcoholism. Edited by Goodwin DW, Teilmann Van Dusen K, Mednick SA. Boston, Kluwer-Nijhoff, 1984

73. Gabrielli WF, Mednick SA, Volavka J, et al: Electroencephalograms in children of alcoholic fathers. Psychophysiology 19:404–407, 1982

74. Pollock VE, Volavka J, Goodwin DW, et al: The EEG after alcohol administration in men at risk for alcoholism. Arch Gen Psychiatry 40:857–861, 1983

75. Drejer K, Theilgaard A, Teasdale T, et al: A prospective study of young men at high risk for alcoholism: neuropsychological assessment. Br J Psychiatry Alcoholism: Clinical and Experimental Research 9:498–502, 1985

76. Volavka J, Pollock V, Gabrielli WF, et al: The EEG in persons at risk for alcoholism, in Currents in Alcoholism (Volume 8). Edited by Gallanter M. New York, Grune and Stratton (in press)

77. Goodwin DW: Studies of familial alcoholism: a growth industry, in Longitudinal Research in Alcoholism. Edited by Goodwin DW, Teilmann Van Dusen K, Mednick SA. Boston, Kluwer-Nijhoff, 1984

78. Lund C, Landesman-Dwyer S: Pre-delinquent and disturbed adolescents: the role of parental alcoholism, in Currents in Alcoholism. Edited by Galanter M. New York, Grune and Stratton, 1979

79. Goodwin DW, Schulsinger F, Hermansen L, et al: Alcoholism and the hyperactive child syndrome. J Nerv Ment Dis 160:349–353, 1975

80. Tarter RE: Childhood hyperactivity and risk for alcoholism. Presented at the annual meeting of the American Psychiatric Association, Los Angeles, May 1984

81. Wood D, Wender P, Reimherr F: The prevalence of attention deficit disorder, residual type, or minimal brain dysfunction in a population of male alcoholic patients. Psychiatry 140:95–98, 1983

82. Morrison J, Stewart M: The psychiatric status of the legal families of adopted hyperactive children. Arch Gen Psychiatry 130:791–792, 1973

83. Cantwell D: Psychiatric illness in the families of hyperactive children. Arch Gen Psychiatry 27:414–417, 1973

84. Alterman AI, Tarter RE, Baughman TH, et al: A comparison of alcoholics high and low in childhood hyperactivity. Presented at the annual meeting of the International Society for Biological Research in Alcoholism, Santa Fe, NM, June 1984

85. Schuckit MA, Chiles JA: Family history as a diagnostic aid in two samples of adolescents. J Nerv Ment Dis 166:165–176, 1978

86. Schuckit MA, Petrich H, Chiles J: Hyperactivity: diagnostic confusion. J Nerv Ment Dis 166:79–87, 1978

87. Steward MA, Leone L: A family study of unsocialized aggressive boys. Biol Psychiatry 13:107–117, 1978

2

Computed Tomography Correlates in Alcoholism

Terry L. Jernigan, Ph.D.
Adolf Pfefferbaum, M.D.
Leslie M. Zatz, M.D.

2

Computed Tomography
Correlates in Alcoholism

With the development of in vivo brain imaging techniques, it is now possible to make observations of the living brain in chronic diseases such as alcoholism. Here, the results of studies of the structure of the brain, as visualized with computed tomography (CT), are presented. An attempt is made to give the reader a sense of the nature and extent of these abnormalities in alcoholic patients and to point out some preliminary notions about their relationship to normal aging, intellectual deficits, and a few clinical variables.

PREVIOUS STUDIES

Computed tomography studies of brain morphology in alcoholics have often demonstrated both significant increases in cortical atrophy and enlargement of the ventricles. In addition, cerebellar atrophy has also been noted (1, 2). Cortical atrophy appears on CT as widening of the fluid-filled cortical sulci. Traditionally, it has been assessed subjectively using two- to four-point scales of the degree of atrophy (3, 4) or objectively by direct linear measurement of sulcal size on polaroid photos or the X-ray film of the CT scan (5).

Figure 1 illustrates the appearance of this abnormality on CT scans. Sections from the high convexity of the cortical surface are shown. Both sections are from subjects who participated in a study of alcoholism (6). The one on the left was taken from the scan of the normal control who had the most sulcal fluid at this level. The one on the right was taken from the alcoholic subject with the most sulcal fluid on this section. Observations of differences of this magnitude are typical. These CT findings are consistent with those of an earlier pneumoencephalographic study (7), classical autopsy observations (8, 9), and recent quantitative pathological studies that involve measurement of pericerebral space (10).

Computed tomography data on alcoholics have also revealed increases in the size of the cerebral ventricular system (3–5, 11–13). Enlarged ventricular size in alcoholics has typically been assessed either by application of atrophy rating scales or by linear measurements across various landmarks in the ventricular system, expressed as ratios of the inner skull diameter. These ventric-

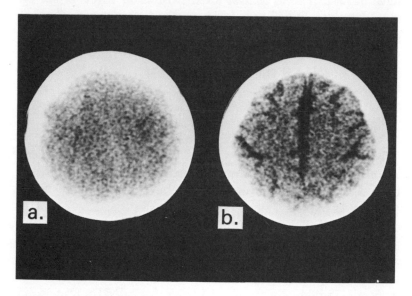

Figure 1. Sections from the high convexity of the cortical surface, on which cortical atrophy is depicted by computed tomography as widening of the fluid-filled cortical sulci. On the left is a scan from a normal subject; on the right, a scan from an alcoholic subject.

ular changes, as well as increases in sulcal size, are very similar to those seen in advancing age. Data from alcoholic subjects must be compared with data from age-matched controls or against age norms. Of interest are the extent to which atrophic changes in the alcoholic brain exceed those expected for the nonalcoholic brain of the same age and the age at which excess atrophy in alcoholics begins to make its appearance. Some CT studies of younger alcoholics have failed to demonstrate significant levels of abnormality (14).

Other considerations in reviewing CT studies of alcoholism relate to the clinical severity and duration of the disease and whether cognitive deficits appear coincident with morphological abnormalities. Although several studies have demonstrated an association between CT changes and cognitive deficits (2–4, 15), or between CT changes and other characteristics of alcoholics (amount of alcohol used, liver status) (2, 16), design considerations have made it hard to control for the common effects of age on these variables. In addition, it has not been clear to what extent factors such as liver disease, hydration, and nutritional status are instrumental in producing the reported abnormalities.

PALO ALTO STUDIES

Brain Measurements

Before the results of studies conducted at the Palo Alto Veteran's Administration Medical Center in California can be presented, a brief description of the methods we have used to study brain structure is in order.

These methods are rather unusual because rather than measure or clinically rank the filmed or printed images, we estimate areas and volumes of tissue and fluid from the numbers underlying each CT image. A CT section consists of a matrix of volume units or pixels, the dimensions of which are typically 1.5 mm × 1.5 mm in the axial plane, with section thickness of 10 mm. Each pixel thus represents a small segment of brain and carries a numerical value on an arbitrary scale (Hounsfeld Units). These numbers represent absorption radiodensity and reflect the proportion of fluid, tissue, or bone in that pixel. We have developed automated algorithms to assess the proportion of fluid and tissue in each pixel from its numerical value.

Semiautomated analyses are performed to divide the CT sections into separate brain areas and compute local fluid volumes. Figure 2 illustrates a typical set of CT sections schematically, as well as the result of our division of the peripheral from the medial areas. The matrix values corresponding to skull bone and areas outside the head are eliminated. In our early studies, the remaining pixel values were evaluated relative to the mean value of a sample from apparently normal brain tissue. Recent modifications of our methods include the addition of digital filtering techniques to reduce the effects of certain artifacts and a new method of separating fluid areas from brain areas without comparison with a sample of brain tissue. The estimated fluid volumes from separate areas are summed to obtain measures of certain fluid structures, such as the ventricular system; or to estimate the degree of cortical

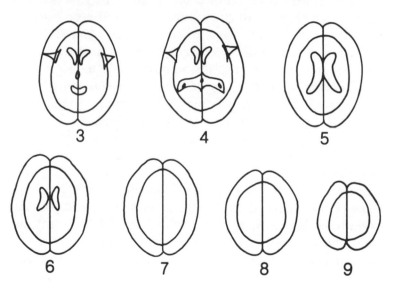

Figure 2. Division of the peripheral from the medial areas in a typical set of computed tomography sections.

atrophy, for example, by voluming sulcal fluid on the brain's convexity.

Study 1

The first study of brain structure in alcoholics at the Palo Alto Veterans Administration Medical Center was completed in 1982 (6). Concurrently, we were collecting data about normal brain structure in aging. As a part of the latter study, we had obtained CT scans in 125 normal volunteers. Our results suggested that increased intracranial fluid volumes occurred with greater frequency and severity in normal individuals over the age of 60 years (17). Dramatic increases in the range of these volumes occurred in the older groups. Figure 3 shows the relationship between age and the estimated ventricular volumes and volumes of convexity sulcal fluid in these normal subjects. Curves were fit to the data to describe the change in the mean volumes across the age range, using polynomial regression analyses. Two sources of variation in the volumes were taken into account in these analyses: head size, which is correlated with the volumes (17), and age. Three age terms were entered into the regression equation to yield a very good fit to the nonlinear change in the average volumes. Because the variance of the volumes also seemed clearly to change with age, a similar polynomial age regression was computed for the standard deviation of the volumes. Both mean and variance increases were highly statistically significant. These results in normal aging were used in our studies of alcoholics to more accurately estimate the degree of abnormality resulting from alcoholism per se.

As mentioned, the aging studies indicated that both the average degree of atrophy and the variability among the subjects increased with advancing age. We therefore needed a method for comparing the alcoholic patients to appropriate controls taking both of these factors into account. Our measures were computed in the following way. Each estimated volume was converted to a z score by subtraction of the predicted volume for the subject's age (obtained from the regression curve for the mean) and division by the

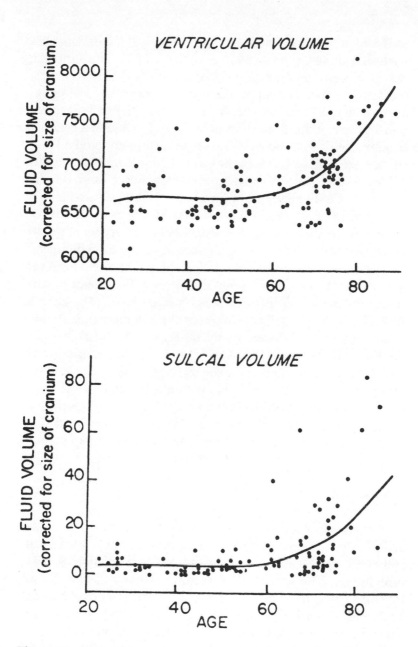

Figure 3. Relationship among age, the estimated ventricular volumes, and volumes of convexity sulcal fluid in normal subjects.

predicted standard deviation of the volume (obtained from the regression curve for the standard deviation). This yields a measure that is corrected for normal aging because only data from normal subjects were used to compute the regression curves. By definition, a group of these z scores taken from normal subjects will have a mean of zero. If the alcoholic patients have an abnormal degree of atrophy, their mean z score will be significantly greater than zero, and the age of the subjects in the group will not affect the results.

Measures of ventricular volume, vertex sulcal fluid volume, and sulcal fluid volume from lower parts of the convexity were compared in 46 chronic alcoholics and 31 controls. No subjects had neurological abnormalities, liver disease, or history of significant head trauma. The group difference in ventricular volume fell just short of significance. All sulcal fluid volumes, however, showed highly significant group differences. The degree of variability in sulcal widening that was observed among the chronic alcoholics was very striking. Many of the patients' scans showed no atrophy at all, whereas many others showed marked sulcal fluid increases that were far outside of the normal range. In this initial study, an attempt was made to estimate roughly the number of years that each patient had been alcohol dependent. These measures did not predict the degree of sulcal widening or ventricular enlargement. Quantitatively, the degree of sulcal widening seen in the 40- to 60-year-old chronic alcoholics in this study resembled that seen in the 70- to 90-year-old normal subjects.

Study 2

We recently completed a second study of chronic alcoholic patients. In this study, a variety of medical, neuropsychological, and other clinical variables were measured in addition to brain morphology. The subjects were recruited from a 30-day alcohol treatment program. They met *Diagnostic and Statistical Manual of Mental Disorders (Third Edition) (DSM-III;* 18) criteria for alcohol dependence and were screened for other medical, neurological, or psychiatric disorders. Their ages ranged from 26 to 65 years. Controls were a group of adult volunteers from the community with low alcohol consumption, otherwise screened using the same criteria.

An alcohol use questionnaire (19) was used to assess alcohol dependence, and lifetime alcohol consumption was estimated from responses to a structured interview. Measures were taken of admission height and weight, weight at time of evaluation, and mean lifetime adult weight. Weight change from mean adult weight to admission weight was also computed.

Brain scans were obtained between 11 and 63 days after the last drink, as reported in the intake interview. Most of the subjects were scanned during the third and fourth weeks of abstinence.

The methods used to quantify atrophy on the CT scans were similar to those used in Study 1 but were modified as described above. The results for the measure of vertex sulcal size are illus-trated in Figure 4. As a group, the alcoholics had significantly enlarged sulci for their age. In the figure, the curve fitting the data collected from the normal controls is plotted, and two standard deviation lines on either side surround it. The curve fitting the data from the alcoholic subjects is also plotted. As can be seen on the sulcal measure, the values for the alcoholics are abnormal relative to the controls across the entire age range. Although the curve relating age to the sulcal volumes in the normal subjects is quite nonlinear, that for the alcoholic patients is approximately parallel to it and significantly higher. In contrast, ventricular en-largement, which is significantly abnormal in the group as a whole, is not present in the younger alcoholics, but becomes increasingly prevalent in the older alcoholics (Figure 5).

In these data, as in the earlier data, great variability is present within the alcoholic group. Even some of the older alcoholics have values low in the normal range, whereas many others showed marked abnormalities. To attempt to explain some of these differ-ences, the relationship between atrophy measures and the esti-mate of lifetime grams of ethanol/kg was examined. Significant correlations of alcohol consumption with both ventricular ($r = 0.44$, $p < .001$) and sulcal ($r = 0.43$, $p < .01$) enlargement were observed. No correlations were observed, however, between atrophy measures and the time elapsed between the last drink and

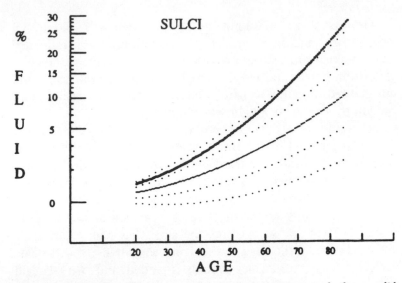

Figure 4. Relationship between age and sulcal size in controls (lower solid curve) and alcoholics (higher solid curve).

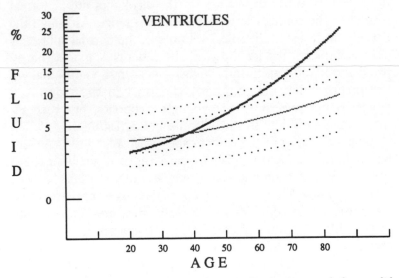

Figure 5. Relationship between age and ventricular size in controls (lower solid curve) and alcoholics (higher solid curve).

the scan; thus, in this sample, no evidence was found for a short-term reduction of the atrophy with continuing abstinence. One suggestive post hoc result was that admission weight showed a significant negative correlation with ventricular size ($r = -0.44$, $p < .001$). The correlation of this variable with the sulcal measure fell far short of significance. The estimate of weight change was also correlated with ventricular size at a similar level. It is possible that weight change reflects compromised nutritional status, and that this factor may mediate brain morphological changes.

Possible Dissociation of Ventricular and Sulcal Changes

Within the alcoholic subjects observed in Study 2, the correlation of the ventricular measure with the measure of vertex cortical atrophy was only 0.25 ($p < .10$). This is a typical degree of association for these two measures in our studies of clinical groups, and experience indicates that significant ventricular enlargement often occurs in the absence of abnormal sulcal widening, and vice versa. The differences in the patterns of observed alcoholic abnormalities across the age range, alluded to previously, also suggest some degree of dissociation of these changes.

Ryan and Butters (19) critically reviewed the premature aging hypothesis of alcoholic brain changes. In their discussion, they suggested that when the neuropsychological deficits (relative to age controls) of alcoholics are of comparable magnitude across the age range (Figure 6), an "accelerated aging" explanation may be offered. In contrast, they argued, neuropsychological deficits that do not appear in younger alcoholic patients but do in older groups, are more suggestive of an "increased vulnerability" interpretation (Figure 7). The latter notion may be taken to mean that as the brain ages it becomes more vulnerable to the toxic effects of alcoholism.

The pattern of the results summarized in Figure 4, for the measure of cortical atrophy, is quite similar to that illustrated in Figure 6, from Ryan and Butters (19). The data suggest that an increased probability of having cortical atrophy is associated with chronic alcoholism regardless of age. The results for ventricular enlargement (Figure 5) much more strongly resemble the pattern described by Ryan and Butters as representing "increasing vulnerability" (Figure 7), and an interaction between age and alcoholism is clearly suggested. It is unlikely that an association of age and increasing duration of alcoholism alone produces this pattern in the ventricular measure because the pattern does not occur in the sulcal data from the same subjects.

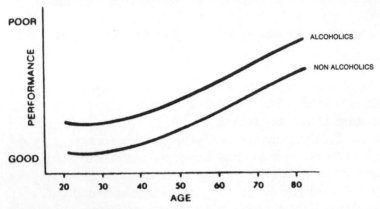

Figure 6. Neuropsychological deficits of alcoholics relative to controls. That the size is comparable across the age range suggests an accelerated aging process.

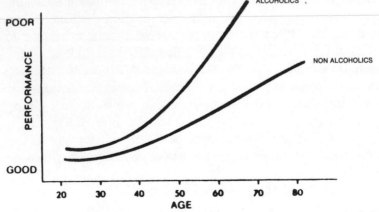

Figure 7. Neuropsychological deficits that do not appear in younger alcoholics but do appear in older alcoholic groups suggest an increased vulnerability of the brain to the toxic effects of alcoholism.

The patterns observed suggest that older alcoholics may be at a greater risk than younger alcoholics to develop ventricular enlargement, and this may represent a somewhat different process than that resulting in cortical atrophy. The fact that the weight variables correlated with ventricular enlargement but did not correlate with cortical atrophy suggests a possible role for nutritional factors. One interesting possibility is that the two types of brain changes may have separate neuropsychological concomitants. In Study II, a series of neuropsychological tests was administered to the alcoholic subjects. Five measures believed to be sensitive to diffuse cerebral dysfunction were examined. Three of these were from the Wechsler Adult Intelligence Scale (WAIS): 1) the difference between the Verbal IQ (VIQ) and Performance IQ (PIQ); 2) the Block Design Scaled Score; and 3) the Digit Symbol Scaled Score. In addition, scores for the associative learning subtest from the Wechsler Memory Scale and the Boston Naming Test were obtained. The correlations of these scores with the ventricular and sulcal measures are presented in Table 1. Except for the correlations with the VIQ-PIQ, the other correlations are partial correlations, controlling for the vocabulary subtest score from the WAIS. The partial correlations are an attempt to increase the power of the analyses by taking an estimate of premorbid intelligence into account. The brain measures are the age-corrected z scores described previously. The use of these z scores removes the mediating effects of normal aging from the correlations.

Correlations between the structural measures and these test scores are, as in other studies, quite modest. Only the block design score shows significant correlations with both brain measures. It

Table 1. Correlations of Test Scores with Ventricular and Sulcal Measures ($N = 34$)

Measures	Verbal/ performance difference	Block design	Digit symbol	Associative learning	Boston Naming Test
Ventricular	.28*	−.33**	−.35***	.15	.20
Sulcral	.00	−.35***	−.21	−.25†	−.06

*$p < .05$. **$p < .03$. ***$p < .02$. †$p < .07$.

may be of some interest that the verbal-performance discrepancy, often considered a general indicator of diffuse cerebral impairment, shows no correlation at all with the sulcal measure despite the fact that moderately severe cortical atrophy was present in this sample. A reverse trend, albeit a very weak one, is observed for the associative learning score. Here correlation is observed between the sulcal measure and the learning score, but there is no sign of any association with the ventricular score. Although the evidence here is extremely weak, it would seem worthwhile to pursue in future studies the possibility that these two kinds of brain structural abnormality are associated with different patterns of cognitive impairment.

CONCLUSION

These studies, like others before them, show clearly that chronic alcoholism is associated with structural abnormalities of the brain. Perhaps the most striking and often reported of these is cortical atrophy, or sulcal widening. Although the mechanism by which this abnormality occurs is not known, some possible associated features have been suggested. A measure of lifetime alcohol consumption predicts the degree of cortical atrophy. Even younger alcoholics, however, who presumably have lower lifetime consumption, show increases over their age controls. The degree of cortical atrophy does seem to be correlated at modest levels with such measures as the block design score and associative learning.

Ventricular enlargement was also demonstrated in the alcoholic groups, but this abnormality seemed only to be present in the older alcoholics, suggesting that perhaps the older patients were more vulnerable in some way. Interestingly, measures of weight at admission and weight change seemed to be associated with ventricular enlargement, suggesting that perhaps nutritional factors play a role in this vulnerability. The estimate of lifetime alcohol consumption also predicted this kind of brain abnormality. Ventricular enlargement was statistically associated with poorer block design and digit symbol scores and a larger discrepancy between the VIQ and PIQ. Although the evidence is not compelling, it is suggested that the two types of brain abnormality examined here may be the result of separate processes, with somewhat different behavioral consequences.

References

1. Wilkinson DA: Examination of alcoholics by computed tomographic (CT) scans: a critical review. Alcoholism 6:31–45, 1982

2. Ron MA: The alcoholic brain: CT scan and psychological findings. Psychological Medicine (Monograph Suppl. 3). Cambridge University Press, Cambridge, 1983

3. Bergman H, Borg S, Hindmarsh T, et al: Computed tomography of the brain and neuropsychological assessment on alcoholic patients. Advances in Medical Biology 126:771–786, 1980a

4. Bergman H, Borg S, Hindmarsh T, et al: Computed tomography of the brain and neuropsychological assessment of male alcoholic patients and a random sample of men from the general male population. Acta Psychiatr Scand 62 (Suppl. 286):47–56, 1980b

5. Fox JH, Ramsey RG, Huckman MS, et al: Cerebral ventricular enlargement: chronic alcoholics examined by computerized tomography. AMA 236:365–368, 1976

6. Jernigan TL, Zatz LM, Ahumada AJ, et al: CT measures of cerebrospinal fluid volume in alcoholics and normal volunteers. Psychiatry Res 7:9–17, 1982

7. Brewer C, Perrett L. Brain damage due to alcohol consumption: an airencephalographic, psychometric, and electroencephalographic study. Br J Addict 66:170–181, 1971

8. Courville C. The Effects of Alcohol on the Nervous System of Man. Los Angeles, San Lucas Press, 1955

9. Victor M, Adams RD, Collins GH. The Wernicke-Korsakoff syndrome. Contemporary Neurology Series, Blackwell, Oxford, 1971

10. Harper C, Kril J. Brain atrophy in chronic alcoholic patients: a quantitative pathological study. J Neurol, Neurosurg, Psychiatry 48:211–217, 1985

11. Carlen PL, Wilkinson DA, Wortzman G, et al: Cerebral atrophy and functional deficits in alcoholics without clinically apparent liver disease. Neurology 31:377–385, 1981

12. Cala LA, Jones B, Mastaglia FL, et al: Brain atrophy and intellectual impairment in heavy drinkers: a clinical psychometric and computed tomography study. Aust NZ J Med 8:147–153, 1978

13. Cala LA, Jones B, Wiley B, et al: A computerized axial tomography (CAT) study of alcohol induced cerebral atrophy in conjunction with other correlates. Acta Psychiatr Scand 62 (Suppl 286):31–40, 1980

14. Hill SY, Mikhael M: Computed tomography scans of alcoholics: cerebral atrophy? Science 24:1237–1238, 1979

15. Graff-Radford NR, Heaton RK, Earnest MP, et al: Brain atrophy and neuropsychological impairment in young alcoholics. J Stud Alcohol 43:859–868, 1982

16. Acker W, Aps EJ, Majumdar SK, et al: The relationship between brain and liver damage in chronic alcoholic patients. J Neurol, Neurosurg, Psychiatry 45:984–987, 1982

17. Zatz LM, Jernigan TL, Ahumada AJ: Changes on computed cranial tomography with aging: intracranial fluid volume. AJNR 3:1–11, 1982

18. American Psychiatric Association: Diagnostic and Statistical Manual of Mental Disorders (Third Edition). Washington, DC, American Psychiatric Association, 1980

19. Skinner HA, Allen BA. Alcohol dependence syndrome: measurement and validation. J Abnorm Psychol 91:199–209, 1982

20. Ryan C, Butters N: Alcohol consumption and premature aging: a critical review, in Recent Developments in Alcoholism (Volume 3). Edited by Galanter M. New York, Plenum Press, 1985

3

Intermediate-Duration (Subacute) Organic Mental Disorder of Alcoholism

Igor Grant, M.D.
Kenneth M. Adams, Ph.D.
Robert Reed, M.S.

3

Intermediate-Duration (Subacute) Organic Mental Disorder of Alcoholism

It is generally accepted that at least some alcoholics suffer cognitive decline and brain damage after many years of alcohol abuse. What is less clear is the extent to which cognitive and structural brain recovery can occur in alcoholics who quit drinking permanently or at least for very extended periods of time. In this chapter, emerging evidence on abstinence-related reversibility is reviewed, and it is contended that at least some of the cognitive and even neuroradiologically determined structural impairments in recently detoxified alcoholics represent not permanent brain damage but rather a slowly resolving intermediate-duration (subacute) organic mental disorder. First, to set the stage for consideration of this topic, we briefly describe the present understanding of the relationship between alcoholism and brain function and structure.

Although it has been appreciated since antiquity that chronic alcoholism can have a deleterious effect on health and behavior, it was not until the late 1800s that a clear association was found between alcohol abuse and brain pathology. Wernicke (1) reported autopsy findings of three cases of a rapidly progressive delirium

Support for this study was provided in part by award SA 325 from the Medical Research Service of the U.S. Veterans Administration to Dr. Igor Grant.

The authors are grateful to Ms. Debi Taylor for her expert assistance in the preparation of this chapter.

associated with ophthalmoplegia and ataxia. Two of the patients were severe alcoholics, and the third suffered from acute starvation resulting from sulfuric acid poisoning. Wernicke found hemorrhagic lesions in the gray matter surrounding the sylvian aqueduct, as well as the third and fourth ventricles.

In 1887 Korsakoff reported a related alcoholism-determined syndrome, characterized by amnesia and a confabulation. Not until almost 85 years later was the continuity between Korsakoff's syndrome and the delirious-ophthalmoplegic-ataxic syndrome discovered by Wernicke clearly established: In 1971 Victor et al. (2) showed that thiamin deficiency represented the underpinning of the Wernicke-Korsakoff syndrome, yet thiamin treatment was not equally efficacious in reversing all of the signs of that disorder. For example, ophthalmoplegia and delirium cleared rapidly, whereas amnesia, some residual confusion, ataxia, and peripheral neuropathy responded only slowly and to an incomplete degree. The pathology of the Wernicke-Korsakoff syndrome is now known to include cell loss in the periaqueductal and periventricular gray sometimes accompanied by punctate hemorrhages. The mammillary bodies are usually affected, as is the dorsomedial nucleus of the thalamus. Recently, histopathological studies of the area of the nucleus basalis of Meynert (including the medial septal nucleus, the nucleus of the diagonal band of Broca, and nucleus basalis cells in the substantia innominata) revealed a 47% loss of cells in this area, which is thought to be one of the principal sites of origin of cholinergic neurons (3). Cell loss in the nucleus basalis of Meynert has also been reported in Alzheimer's disease, another condition in which amnesia is prominent.

Additional uncommon complications whose neuroanatomical basis has been clarified include central pontine myelinolysis and Marchiafava-Bignami disease. The former is characterized by "a single symmetrical focus of demyelination in the center of the basis pontis" (2, p. 142). The lesion is sometimes asymptomatic, but can be fatal presenting with spastic paralysis of the lower cranial nerves, and quadriplegia. Marchiafava-Bignami disease is characterized by "symmetrical degeneration of myelin . . . of the central portion of the corpus callosum" (2, p. 143).

The profound retrograde and anterograde amnesia that characterizes the Wernicke-Korsakoff syndrome is relatively uncommon. Indeed, investigators now tend to believe that the Wernicke-Korsakoff syndrome does not represent end-stage alcoholic brain disease but rather the superimposition of a thiamin deficiency onto a chronic neurotoxic process related to ethanol itself (4). Both neuropsychological and neuranatomic lines of evidence support this distinction.

From a neuropsychological standpoint, the memory deficits of Korsakoff and non-Korsakoff alcoholics differ considerably. Although both groups show anterograde memory loss (that is, difficulty in learning new material), this deficit is more profound in Korsakoff patients. More important, the retrograde amnesia of the Korsakoff patient can be very severe, whereas that of non-Korsakoff alcoholics tends to range from mild to nonexistent. For example, non-Korsakoff alcoholics tend to have good memory of autobiographical events, whereas Korsakoff alcoholics show profound memory gaps and confabulation. The other neuropsychological changes appear to be common to both groups of alcoholics. For example, many (perhaps 50% or more) chronic alcoholics who have been abstinent approximately one month show deficits in abstract reasoning, problem solving, complex perceptual motor abilities, and divided attention in addition to the aforementioned memory difficulties. Alternatively, general intelligence as measured by verbal IQ, as well as language skills, tends to be preserved even in severe alcoholism.

The neuropathology of non-Korsakoff alcoholism is still imperfectly characterized. Courville (5) stated that alcoholism was "the most common cause of cerebral cortical atrophy in the fifth and sixth decades of life. It may appear as early as the first few years of the fourth decade, particularly in individuals who have presented signs of a psychotic trend" (p. 46). As to gross pathology, Courville stated, "the characteristic change consists of a fairly uniform atrophy of the convolutions of the upper part of the dorsolateral surface of the frontal lobes, not necessarily to the same extent in both hemispheres. This process extends to the middle and lower frontal convolutions, then to the pre- and postcentral gyri, and finally into the superior parietal lobule. . . . The convolutions of the temporal lobe, the inferior parietal lobe, the occipital lobe, and the medial and basilar surfaces of the cerebral hemispheres are usually spared" (p. 46). Courville also noted a variable degree of ventricular dilation and cerebellar atrophy.

Courville's observations have been confirmed by computed tomography (CT) scans of the brain. Over 20 CT studies of alcoholics and social drinkers have appeared since the mid-1970s (6–8; also see Chapter 2 of this monograph). The prevalence of abnormal CT findings has ranged from 7% to 100%. Commonalities in the data suggest that perhaps half of recently detoxified alcoholics show some degree of sulcal widening and that this phenomenon can be observed to some degree in alcoholics of all ages. Ventricular dilatation occurs somewhat less frequently, perhaps in a third of cases. It is not evident in most patients under 40 years of age but increases in prominence in aging alcoholics (see Chapter 2 of this monograph).

REVERSIBILITY OF IMPAIRMENT

From the standpoint of time course, reversibility can be considered to occur in three phases: acute, short term, and long term. Until recently most of the literature has focused on the acute and short-term phases.

The acute phase comprises the hours and days during which initial recovery from an alcoholic bout takes place. In this period tremulousness, sleep disturbance, irritability, mild confusion, and distractability may occur. In severe cases full blown delirium tremens can occur, heralded within the first 24 hours by a convulsion and proceeding to confusion, severe tremulousness, marked agitation, vivid visual hallucinations, and various signs of automatic instability. Untreated, this syndrome can, in rare instances, be fatal; with treatment, the syndrome generally resolves within a week. Neuropsychological testing during this acute (but nondelirious) phase generally shows considerable deficit, particularly on tests requiring sustained attention, abstract reasoning, perceptual motor integration, and learning.

By the third or fourth week of continuous abstinence, most patients show significant recovery in these neuropsychological measures; in many instances, however, performance is still impaired relative to age- and education-matched controls (9–11). During this short-term recovery phase, two mechanisms of neuropsychological improvement occur: time-dependent recovery and experience-dependent recovery (12, 13). *Time-dependent recovery* refers to the improvement in performance on certain neuropsychological tests as a function of the passage of time. For example, alcoholics improve considerably in their performance on the digit symbol substitution task of the Wechsler Adult Intelligence Scale (WAIS) from the first through the fourth week of abstinence. Such improvement is not simply due to "practice," because groups of alcoholics who have never taken the test before but who have been abstinent for four weeks perform better than do groups of alcoholics who are tested in the first week. Experience-dependent recovery appears to require prior exposure to a test in order to demonstrate improvement. Goldman et al. (13) suggested that improvement on Trail Making Part B (an element of the Halstead-Reitan Battery that requires subjects to use a pencil to connect numbers and letters on a piece of paper in the correct alternating order under pressure of time) illustrates this process. According to the Goldman et al. studies, alcoholics who were abstinent four weeks did not perform much better on Trail Making than did alcoholics who were abstinent one week if they had not seen the test before. Alternatively, both alcoholic groups improved to control levels after three exposures to the task. This suggests that some cognitive abilities that may become impaired as a consequence of alcohol abuse stay dormant until activated by appropriate stimulation. The exact mechanisms underlying experience-dependent recovery are not known. It is possible that alcoholics in phases 1 (acute) and 2 (short term) of recovery have difficulties responding to novel problem-solving situations or that anxiety, irritability, or dysphoria, which accompany these stages, contribute to problems in neuropsychological performance. Repeated exposure to a task may attenuate these novelty-related and affect-related inefficiencies.

LONG-TERM RECOVERY

Until relatively recently, most investigators assumed that neuro-psychological recovery was more or less complete after the first three to four weeks of abstinence. Thus, the deficits in abstraction, complex perceptual motor abilities and memory that have been observed in many alcoholics who are sober approximately one month, have been thought to reflect permanent brain damage.

It is now becoming clear that the brain has more potential for recovery than was previously believed. Evidence for this comes from human neuropsychological and neuroradiological studies, as well as morphological studies of the brains of animals subjected to chronic ethanol treatment.

Some of the earliest evidence for long-term recovery of brain function was actually provided by an electroencephalogram (EEG) study. Bennett et al. (14) reported normalization of the EEG during a year or more of detoxification in some alcoholics and persisting mild abnormalities in others. These investigators described their findings as an "intermediate stage of alcoholic brain disease"; however, the meaning they use for the term *intermediate* differs from the meaning we propose in that Bennett et al. were describing a disorder that was midway between a fully reversible acute brain syndrome and an irreversible chronic brain syndrome. The implication was that many cases would go on to permanent brain damage without treatment. We propose that the term *intermediate* be used to mean that this is a phase of slow recovery common to many if not most alcoholics.

Long and McLachlan (15) performed one of the first long-term neuropsychological outcome studies. They examined 17 alcoholics an average of 11 days after cessation of drinking and approximately one year later. No controls were retested. They found improvements on several neuropsychological measures, including Halstead's Category Test, Tactual Performance Test, Tapping Test, and Wechsler-Bellevue Digit Span and Block Design.

Berglund et al. (16) reexamined a group of 53 alcoholics an average of 3.7 years after they received initial treatment. Although many tests showed no significant change, the subjects did perform somewhat better on block design and certain memory tests at follow-up. The authors noted a tendency for those who reported drinking less in the interim to show more improvement. O'Leary and associates (17) also demonstrated a significant neuropsychological improvement in a group of 24 alcoholics who were retested after 12 to 16 months of abstinence (the initial testing was 9 to 14 days after last drink).

Several studies also examined the status of alcoholics three to six months after detoxification. Althought one group found no difference in performance on the WAIS, Graham-Kendall, Trail Making test, and Raven Advanced Matrices between alcoholics who were sober 21 days and those who were sober 110 days (18), another found evidence of improved performance on visual spatial tasks in alcoholics who were abstinent for 11 weeks (19). In Leber et al.'s study, the long-term-abstinent alcoholics were statistically indistinguishable from the controls. In a follow-up study by Guthrie and Elliott (20), alcoholics tested at six months improved in their level of performance at 14 days after the last drink. Ryan and Butters (21) found that alcoholics abstinent an average of eight months performed normally on tests of short-term memory, were slightly impaired on verbal paired associate learning, and were more significantly impaired on a nonverbal learning task (symbol digit paired associate learning).

Several groups have examined alcoholics who have been abstinent for prolonged periods of time (in excess of one year). The study by Berglund et al. (16) has already been mentioned; its results are difficult to interpret because continuing abstinence was not a requisite of that study. Brandt et al. (22) performed tests of learning and memory with three groups of alcoholics composed on the basis of duration of abstinence. One group was abstinent 1 to 2 months; the second, 12 to 36 months; and the third, more than 60 months. The authors found that the very long-term-abstinent group performed significantly better than did those abstinent only one or two months on most tests, including a four-word short-term memory test, symbol digit and digit symbol substitution, and the delayed recognition condition of the Benton Visual Retention test. With the exception of the word memory test, the medium duration abstainers (12 to 36 months) performed in a manner intermediate between the short-term and very long-term abstainers. At the same time, continuing neuropsychological deficit was suggested by the fact that even the very long-term abstainers still performed worse than controls on a nonverbal learning test—symbol digit paired associate learning—and on a perceptual measure—the embedded figures test. These authors concluded that short- and long-term memory differed in their recovery rates. Short-term abstainers had difficulty holding verbal information in temporary storage, but this ability appeared to recover in the long-term. Alternatively, the authors suggested that ability to learn new and novel associations did not recover even with very prolonged abstinence.

Fabian and Parsons (23) performed a detailed neuropsychological examination of women alcoholics who were recently detoxified or abstinent approximately four years. The results of the neuropsychological battery were subjected to factor analysis, and performance in the ability areas summarized by these factors was compared between the two alcoholic groups and a group of nonalcoholic controls. The investigators found that the recently detoxified alcoholics performed worse on a nonverbal-spatial-perceptual motor factor than did controls. The long-term-abstinent alcoholics were statistically indistinguishable from controls, although their score on this factor was intermediate between that of the recently detoxified group and the nonalcoholics.

Since the mid 1970s, our group has been involved in a series of studies of alcoholics and polydrug abusers; specific emphasis has been placed on neuropsychological recoverability. Our initial work was with polysubstance abusers who also abused alcohol. In different studies, subjects were reexamined three to six months after initial testing, which was conducted three to four weeks after detoxification. On the basis of these studies, we suggested that some polysubstance abusers showed evidence of what we termed "an intermediate duration organic mental disorder," which seemed to reverse slowly in the months following abstinence (24–26).

In studies specifically addressing recoverability in alcoholism, we examined a group of younger alcoholics (average age 37 years), some of whom had been abstinent approximately four weeks and others a minimum of 18 months (27). In that study we found that the longer-term abstinent alcoholics were statistically indistinguishable from age- and educated-matched controls on any of the tests comprising the Halstead-Reitan Battery tests, WAIS, and tests of verbal and nonverbal recall.

In a subsequent investigation, we examined larger groups of recently detoxified and long-term-abstinent alcoholics and matched controls. In that study, the age ranged from 25 to 59 years. Blind clinical ratings of neuropsychological test results showed that 41% of the recently detoxified alcoholics were impaired on abstracting ability. This compared with an impairment rate of 21% for the long-term-abstinent alcoholics and 26% for nonalcoholics.

These findings were confirmed in a factor analytic study. Factor analysis is a mathematical way of grouping test data on the basis of shared variance. Our particular study yielded a four-factor solution. The abilities that seemed to be captured by these mathematical factors included verbal language ability, a problem-solving learning dimension, an attentional/alertness dimension, and a simple motor skills dimension. We found that recently detoxified alcoholics performed worse than the long-term-abstinent group and controls on the problem-solving learning factor. Long-term-abstinent alcoholics were indistinguishable from controls. The results of these two studies of younger and mixed-age alcoholics strongly suggest that alcoholics who are able to maintain stable abstinence for long periods of time can have neuropsychological performances which are essentially normal.

However, because these studies were not longitudinal in nature (that is, the same subjects were not followed over time), it is not possible to state categorically that alcoholics improved to a normal level. It is certainly equally possible that those alcoholics who comprised the long-term-abstinent group both in our studies and in those by Fabian and Parsons were simply better functioning in the first instance. It could even be argued that relatively intact neuropsychological abilities in the face of chronic inebriation might have been helpful in allowing some groups of alcoholics to take advantage of treatment programs and thereafter to maintain stable sobriety.

Although we cannot discount this line of reasoning, we have some additional information that suggests processes of long-term recovery are indeed operating. For example, many of the subjects in Grant et al.'s (27) study were followed up and retested after approximately a year (28). At initial testing the previous year, 26% of the recently detoxified alcoholics were impaired compared with 20% of the long-term-abstinent group and 19% of controls. At one-year follow-up, the rate of impairment in the first group rose to 39%, whereas in the second group it fell to 12%. When we examined changes in individual test results, we found that there was greater improvement on many tests in the long-term-abstinent group than in the control group, suggesting that factors other than simple "practice" effect were responsible.

We recently followed up on 156 subjects in a longitudinal study and performed blind clinical ratings of impairment and change on results between first and second testing. The average intertest interval was approximately two years (29).

Table 1 shows the rate of impairment in the three groups at follow-up. One can see that the long-term-abstinent alcoholics were again indistinguishable from controls on the basis of these ratings. Alternatively, subjects who initially had been in the recently detoxified group had an impairment rate of 32.2%.

Table 1. Clinical Rating of Neuropsychological Functioning: Three Groups at Two-Year Follow-Up

Functioning	Recently detoxified alcoholics (%)	Long-term-abstinent alcoholics (%)	Nonalcoholic controls (%)
Clinically unimpaired NP performance	67.8	89.4	88.0
Clinically impaired NP performance	32.2	10.6	12.0

Note. NP = neuropsychological performance.

Even more interesting are the clinical ratings of change. The clinician, who did not know the group membership of subjects whose results he was examining, rated each pair of test results on a five-point scale denoting marked improvement, slight improvement, no change, slight worsening, and substantial worsening. Table 2 displays the results of the clinician's rating of change. The first three groups were composed of alcoholic subjects; the fourth group, nonalcoholic controls. Group 1 contained alcoholics who had resumed drinking in the interim. Virtually all of these alcoholics had originally been in the detoxified group. Group 2 contained alcoholics originally in the recently detoxified group who maintained stable abstinence. Hence, they were abstinent for an average of two years between testings. In Group 3 were alcoholics who began the study having already been abstinent an average of approximately four years. Because all but a few maintained stable abstinence in the two-year follow-up, most subjects were abstinent an average of six years at the time of repeated testing.

Turning first to controls, the rate of clinician-determined improvement was 4%, and the rate of deterioration was 0%. This 4% rate of improvement can be taken to reflect whatever practice effect the clinician was unable to account for in his ratings, plus other sources of unaccounted variability in subject performance or clinician ratings. In Group 3—the alcoholics who entered the study in a state of prolonged abstinence and maintained that abstinence an additional two years—a surprising 19% of subjects were rated as significantly improved. This is a rate five times that

Table 2. Clinical Rating of Change in Neuropsychological Function: Four Groups at Two-Year Follow-Up

	Resumed drinking (%)	Short-term sober (%)	Long-term sober (%)	Nonalcoholic controls (%)
Clinically improved	9	16	19	4
Clinically unchanged	53	64	77	90
Clinically worse	38	20	4	6

seen in controls and suggests that factors other than practice effect and error variance were responsible. There was also modest improvement in the other two alcoholic groups. The rate of improvement in the shorter term abstainers was 16% and in those who resumed drinking, 9%. Thus, even in the face of resumption of some drinking (usually at a lower level), some subjects were able to improve on their previous performance.

The most interesting and novel data are those found for the long-term abstainers. Even after four to six years of abstinence evidence of some continuing recovery was found in a few of the subjects. Whether this neuropsychological improvement reflects further biological recovery of the brain or can be explained by the effects of the experience-dependent learning described earlier is unclear.

In sum, these neuropsychological investigations strongly suggest that a slow reversal of subtle neuropsychological deficit exists over extended periods of time in alcoholics who maintain stable sobriety. It no longer appears justified to assume that essentially all recovery is complete after the first month or so of abstinence. It appears that the longer patients abstain, the more likely it is that their neuropsychological performance will approach that of controls.

NEURORADIOLOGICAL EVIDENCE OF REVERSIBILITY OF BRAIN CHANGES

Prior to the advent of CT, it was not practicable to image the brain repeatedly in an effort to document possible reversible changes.

In 1978, Carlen and associates (30) published a provocative report on CT changes in alcoholics followed up on after prolonged abstinence. Their study involved eight alcoholics who were scanned initially between 2½ to 11 weeks after the last drink and then reexamined after a period of sobriety ranging from 33 to 97 weeks. The authors demonstrated a partially reversible atrophy in 4 of 8 patients. The authors concluded that "reversible atrophy was noted only in those patients who abstained from alcohol, showed clinical improvement, and had their initial CT scans before demonstrable clinical improvement was complete" (p. 77). Although the robustness of these findings (particularly the relationship to interim abstinence) has been questioned (10), the fact remains that Carlen at al. provided what may have been the first morphological support for the early suggestions from the neuropsychological literature that long-term brain improvements can occur.

In a subsequent study, Carlen and Wilkinson (31) reported on 23 alcoholics who were scanned initially within five weeks of their last drink and reexamined two to nine months later. Eleven of the subjects remained abstinent in the interim, 7 decreased their drinking, and five continued drinking at their usual rate after discharge from the hospital. Again, there was a tendency for measures of atrophy to decrease, although not as dramatically as reported earlier. Interestingly, in the abstinent group the authors demonstrated a correlation between the age of the patient and change in sulcal width between testings. This result suggests that reversal of brain shrinkage is most likely to occur in younger abstinent alcoholics.

Ron et al. (32) also followed up on 23 patients from 31 to 91 weeks after their initial scanning as inpatients. Nine of these patients either remained abstinent or had only a few drinks, whereas 14 continued drinking at their preadmission level. Improvements were noted in 4 of the 9 abstinent patients, whereas 3 of the 14 who continued drinking worsened on their CT ratings. In subsequent work, Ron (7) confirmed that there was substantial CT improvement after approximately a one-year follow-up, but indicated that it was difficult to establish reliable associations between abstinence or amount of interscan drinking and degree of CT change. More recent work by Carlen and Wilkinson (33) continues to indicate that there is partial reversibility of cerebral atrophy. In addition, these authors have reported some preliminary observations on increase in cerebral density (as measured by CT absorption numbers) in alcoholics whose CT scans showed some improvement.

Observations with social drinkers also support the notion of a reversible brain shrinkage that can be observed on repeated CT scanning. For example, Cala (34) followed 26 heavy social drinkers (mean daily alcohol consumption of 70 g, which is equivalent to five to six drinks per day) who agreed to abstain completely from alcohol for six months. Twenty-four of these subjects were thought to have CT abnormalities on initial testing. Among these, 16 showed improvement after six months of total abstinence. Cala's study suggests that even those engaged in moderate to heavy drinking in the nonalcoholic range may show some reversible CT changes. Because Cala also reported some neuropsychological deficits in this group, these data can be taken as preliminary evidence that the intermediate duration organic mental disorder observed in alcoholics may also occur in mild form in heavy social drinkers who drink regularly.

Evidence that recent heavy drinking in nonalcoholics can result in CT changes has been presented by Bergman (35). There was a modest but significant relationship between CT abnormality and amount of ethanol consumed during the week before investigation among heavy-drinking men (those whose daily consumption was in excess of 33 g of ethanol). It appeared that CT abnormalities were particularly associated with present drinking (that is, those who had a measurable blood alcohol concentration at time of scanning).

In summary, recent CT studies have suggested that there may be some reversal of sulcal atrophy and ventricular dilatation in alcoholics who reduce drinking or become abstinent. Very preliminary data even suggest that more heavily drinking social drinkers may have CT measured abnormalities that may be associated with amount of recent drinking.

EVIDENCE FOR REVERSIBILITY FROM ANIMAL STUDIES

Animals receiving chronic ethanol treatment (CET) have been used increasingly as a model for the effects of alcohol excess on the brain (36, 37). Chronic ethanol treatment produces reduction in weight of certain regions of the brain, including the hippocampus, thalamus, and midbrain. Certain other areas seem more resistant to CET, including the cerebral cortex, hypothalamus, striatum, pons, and medulla (37). In the brain areas affected, there is a loss of cells and dendrites. For example, four months of CET produced a substantial loss of dendritic spines in hippocampal pyradmidal cells and dentate granule cells (38). Laboratory rats exposed to five months of CET showed a 16% loss of hippocampal pyramidal cells and a 20% loss in granule cells (39).

There is also now some evidence that these neuropathological changes are partially reversible. For example, an interesting report has recently suggested morphometric improvement in the brains of animals two months after cessation of CET (40). In this experiment, rats were fed an ethanol liquid diet for five months. Some were killed immediately, and their brains were studied neuropathologically; others were examined after only two months of being ethanol free. Consistent with previous research, McMullen et al. (40) noted reduced branching in proximal basal dendrites of the hippocampal CA1 pyramidal cells corresponding to a decrease in second-order dendrites. They found no evidence of cell death. In the basilar dendritic regions, there was a reduction in strata thickness, suggesting a loss of afferent fiber connections.

After two months of detoxification, animals who had been subjected to CET were no different morphometrically than were control animals. Specifically, there were no differences in numbers of dendritic spines or strata thickness. The authors concluded that prolonged abstinence is consistent with morphological recovery, assuming no actual cell death had occurred.

Such animal data, if confirmed, may have considerable relevance in understanding some of the human research that was reviewed previously in this chapter. Specifically, thickness of brain regions is probably largely a reflection of the richness of the dendritic field. If this is so, and if chronic exposure to ethanol causes a loss of dendrites, then this would provide a physiological explanation for the development of CT measured shrinkage. Cessation of abusive drinking may allow for dendritic regrowth, which could then explain increased thickness of the brain substance (that is, the reversal of CT measured atrophy).

CONCLUSIONS

Neuropsychologic, neuroradiologic, and animal studies are increasingly converging on the observation that there may be long-term recovery of brain function and structure as a correlate of prolonged abstinence from abusive alcohol consumption. The neuropsychologic data suggest that there may be three phases of recovery. The first phase may last a few hours to approximately a week; it consists of early physiologic readjustments to discontinuation of ethanol. The behavioral indicators of the first phase range from irritability, dysphoria, inattentiveness, and disruption of sleep to frank delirium, convulsions, and major autonomic disturbances.

The second phase of recovery spans the next several weeks of stable abstinence. This phase can begin as early as a few hours or days after cessation of drinking and may be characterized initially by mild to moderate neuropsychologic deficits. These deficits include difficulties in novel problem solving, abstracting ability, and reasoning. They can also include defects in perceptual motor skills and in learning and remembering. By the fourth week of abstinence, considerable improvement is likely to occur, although in many alcoholics subtle deficits will continue to be uncovered.

The third phase of recovery may require months to years to take full effect. During this period, the highest level of cognitive skills (those involved in abstract reasoning and new learning) gradually return to normal. In some alcoholics, even those with very extensive histories of drinking and modest impairments in the first two phases, total recovery apparently can occur, at least from a behavioral standpoint. In others, deficits of varying degrees of severity will continue to be demonstrated. Those who demonstrate such deficits have probably entered the fourth stage, which entails chronic, mild, stable cognitive dysfunction.

At present, there is no generally agreed-upon nosology that encompasses the phenomena that we have described. In the *Diagnostic and Statistical Manual of Mental Disorders (DSM-III;* 41), seven organic mental disorders are attributed to the ingestion of alcohol (see Table 3). It is readily apparent that none of these categories captures the neurobehavioral state of many alcoholics in their middle and later phases of abstinence.

The gap in present nosology falls between the *DSM-III* category of alcohol "withdrawal delirium" and "dementia associated with alcoholism." To bridge this gap and thus characterize a large group of alcoholics, we propose that the psychiatric taxonomy embrace two additional entities. These categories would be "intermediate duration organic mental disorder associated with alcoholism" (or other substance abuse) and "subacute dementia." Some proposed criteria for each of these diagnoses are presented in Tables 4, 5, and 6.

"Intermediate duration organic mental disorder" is meant to cover clinical phenomena observed between the end of phase one of recovery (that is, end of acute withdrawal) and the reestablishment of the best attainable level of cognitive function after prolonged abstinence. "Subacute dementia" describes the condition of alcoholics who have mild to moderate stable cognitive deficits that are not severe enough to qualify under *DSM-III* diagnostic criteria for dementia. For example, persons with subacute dementia might not have a "loss of intellectual abilities of sufficient severity to interfere with social or occupational functioning" (41, p. 111). At the very least, such psychosocial impairment might be so subtle as not to be discernable under ordinary circumstances. For example, a recovered alcoholic accountant might have no difficulties whatever preparing tax returns or performing well-learned computa-

Table 3. Seven Organic Mental Disorders Attributable to the Ingestion of Alcohol in *DSM-III*

Alcohol intoxication

Alcohol idiosyncratic intoxication

Alcohol withdrawal

Alcohol withdrawal delirium

Alcohol hallucinosis

Alcohol amnestic disorder

Dementia associated with alcoholism

Note. DSM-III = Diagnostic and Statistical Manual of Mental Disorders (Third Edition) (41).

Table 4. Diagnostic Criteria for Intermediate Duration Organic Mental Disorder Associated With Alcohol Abuse and Alcoholism

Presumptive diagnosis

1. Neuropsychiatric disorder[a] is evident following prolonged heavy ingestion of ethanol.

2. Disorder is evident as early as the first week of abstinence and persists for months or even several years after cessation of alcohol ingestion.

3. Disorder is not due to other causes of slowly reversible organic mental disorder (for example, head injury, hypothyroidism).

Definitive diagnosis

4. Repeated evaluations show improvement in neuropsychiatric disorder in relation to abstinence or reduced consumption.

[a] For our definition of neuropsychiatric disorder, see Table 6.

Table 5. Diagnostic Criteria for Subacute Dementia Associated With Alcohol Abuse or Alcoholism

Presumptive diagnosis

1. Neuropsychiatric disorder[a] is evident following prolonged heavy ingestion of ethanol.

2. Disorder is evident a minimum of one year after cessation of alcohol ingestion.

3. Disorder is not due to other causes of subacute dementia (for example, late sequaele of head injury, permanent effects of hypothyroidism).

Definitive diagnosis

4. Repeated evaluations show no significant improvement in neuropsychiatric disorder in relation to stable abstinence beyond one year.

[a] For our definition of neuropsychiatric disorder, see Table 6.

Table 6. Definition of Neuropsychiatric Disorder

A. Subjective sense of reduced intellectual acuity or capacity (for example, a sense that it is more difficult to learn new things, to remember, to handle more complex information)

B. One of the following objective signs:

1. Neuropsychological deficit (for example, abstracting ability, perceptual motor skills, memory below expectations for age- and education-matched controls)

2. Computed tomography or magnetic resonance scan evidence of abnormally widened sulci or ventricular dilatation compared with age-matched norms

3. Electroencephalogram evidence of diffuse disturbance (for example, slowing of alpha, increase in theta activity)

tions. He or she might, however, have mild difficulties in abstracting ability and problem solving, which would become evident only if he or she were promoted to some higher level of responsibility. This same individual might not have any significant memory impairment. Yet on neuropsychological testing he or she might show mild deficits in performance on such tests as Category, Wisconsin Card Sort, or conceptual analogies. It would clearly be inappropriate to classify such a person as in the "frankly demented" as that term is used in *DSM-III*. It would be equally inappropriate to overlook subtle, stable cognitive deficits that although not interfering with ordinary functioning, might nevertheless indicate a persisting organic mental disorder.

In conclusion, we present evidence for the existence of a slowly reversing intermediate duration organic mental disorder associated with stable abstinence from alcohol among alcoholics. This gradually resolving disorder may take months to years to reach full recovery. We suggest criteria for the diagnosis of this disorder. In addition, we suggest that many long-term abstinent alcoholics show evidence of a mild, stable cognitive deficit, which we call subacute dementia, that is not of sufficient severity to qualify for *DSM-III* diagnosis of alcoholic dementia. Finally, we suggest that prevalence of permanent brain damage and neuropsychologic deficit in alcoholics might have been overestimated because the condition of subjects at the end of a period of hospitalization for detoxification and rehabilitation was assumed to be valid as a permanent state. The delineation of the intermediate duration organic mental disorder suggests that the prevalence of permanent brain damage in relation to alcoholism can be discerned only through studies of alcoholics who have maintained stable abstinence for prolonged periods of time.

References

1. Wernicke C: Lehrbuch der Gehirnkrankheiten fur Aerzte und Studirende. Theodor Fisher, Kassel u. Berlin, 2:229–242, 1881

2. Victor M, Adams RD, Colins GH: The Wernicke-Korsakoff Syndrome. Philadelphia, F.A. Davis, 1971

3. Arendt T, Bigl V, Arendt A, et al: Loss of neurons in the nucleus basalis of Meynert in Alzheimer's disease, paralysis agitans and Korsakoff's disease. Acta Neuropathol 61:101–108, 1983

4. Butters N, Brandt J: The continuity hypothesis: the relationship of long-term alcoholism to the Wernicke-Korsakoff syndrome, in Recent Developments in Alcoholism (Volume 3). Edited by Galanter M. New York, Plenum Press, 1985

5. Courville CB: Effects of Alcohol on the Nervous System of Man. Los Angeles, San Lucas Press, 1955

6. Ishii T: A comparison of cerebral atrophy in CT scan findings among alcoholic groups. Acta Psychiatr Scand 309 (Suppl): 7–30, 1983

7. Ron MA: The alcoholic brain: CT scan and psychological findings. Psychological Medicine, Monograph Supplement 3. Cambridge: Cambridge University Press, 1983

8. Wilkinson DA: Examination of alcoholics by computed tomographic (CT) scans: a critical review. Alcoholism: Clinical and Experimental Research 6:31–45, 1982

9. Grant I: The brain and alcohol: neuropsychological correlates. J Consult Clin Psychol (in press)

10. Grant I, Reed R: Neuropsychology of alcohol and drug abuse, in Substance Abuse and Psychopathology. Edited by Alterman AI New York, Plenum Press, 1985

11. Parsons OA, Farr SD: The neuropsychology of alcohol and drug use, in Handbook of Clinical Neuropsychology. Edited by Filskov SB, Boll TS. New York, Wiley, 1981

12. Goldman MS: Cognitive impairment in chronic alcoholics: some cause for optimism. Am Psychol 38:1045–1054, 1983

13. Goldman MS, Klisz DK, William DL: Experience-dependent recov-

ery of cognitive functioning in young alcoholics. Addict Behav 10:169–176, 1985

14. Bennett AE, Mowery GL, Fort JT: Brain damage from chronic alcoholism: the diagnosis of intermediate stage of alcoholic brain disease. Am J Psychiatry 116:705–711, 1960

15. Long, JA McLachlan JFC: Abstract reasoning and perceptual motor efficiency in alcoholics. Quarterly Journal of Studies on Alcohol 35:1220–1229, 1974

16. Berglund M, Gustafson L, Hagberg B et al: Cerebral dysfunction in alcoholism and presenile dementia. A comparison of two groups with similar reduction of the cerebral blood flow. Acta Psychiatr Scand 55:391–398, 1977

17. O'Leary MR, Donovan MA, Chaney EF: The relationship of perceptual field orientation to measures of cognitive functioning and current adaptive abilities in alcoholics and nonalcoholics. J Nerv Ment Dis 165:275–282, 1977

18. Kish GB, Hagen JM, Woody MM et al: Alcoholics' recovery from cerebral impairment as a function of duration of abstinence. J Clin Psychol 36:584–589, 1980

19. Leber WR, Jenkins RL, Parsons OA: Recovery of visual-spatial learning and memory in chronic alcoholics. J Clin Psychol 37:192–197, 1981

20. Guthrie A, Elliott WA: The nature and reversibility of cerebral impairment in alcoholism: treatment implications. J Stud Alcohol 41:1 147–155, 1980

21. Ryan C, Butters N: Learning and memory impairments in young and old alcoholics: evidence for the premature aging hypothesis. Alcoholism: Clinical and Experimental Research 4:288–293, 1980

22. Brandt J, Butters N, Ryan C, et al: Cognitive loss and recovery in long-term alcohol abusers. Arch Gen Psychiatry 40:435–442, 1983

23. Fabian MS, Parsons OA: Differential improvements of cognitive

functions in recovering alcoholic women. J Abnorm Psychol 92:81–95, 1983

24. Grant I, Judd L: Neuropsychological and EEG disturbances in polydrug users. Am J Psychiatry 133:1039–1042, 1976

25. Grant I, Adams K, Carlin A, et al: The collaborative neuropsychological study of polydrug users. Arch Gen Psychiatry 35:1063–1074, 1978

26. Judd LL, Grant I: Intermediate duration organic mental disturbance among polydrug abusing patients. Psychiatr Clin North Am 1(1): 153–167, 1978

27. Grant I, Adams K, Reed R: Normal neuropsychological abilities of alcoholic men in their late thirties. Am J Psychiatry 136:10, 1263–1269, 1979

28. Adams K, Grant I, Reed R: Neuropsychology in alcoholic men in their late thirties: one year follow-up. Am J Psychiatry 137:928–931, 1980

29. Grant I, Adams KM, Reed R: Aging, abstinence, and medical risk factors in the prediction of neuropsychologic deficit among long-term alcoholics. Arch Gen Psychiatry 41:710–718, 1984

30. Carlen PL, Wortzman G, Holgate RC, et al: Reversible cerebral atrophy in recently abstinent chronic alcoholics measured by computed tomography scans. Science 200:1076–1078, 1978

31. Carlen PL, Wilkinson DA: Alcoholic brain damage and reversible deficits. Acta Psychiatr Scand 62:103–118, 1980

32. Ron MA, Acker W, Lishman WA: Morphological abnormalities in the brains of chronic alcoholics: a clinical, psychological and computerized axial tomographic study. Acta Psychiatr Scand 62:41–46, 1980

33. Carlen PL, Wilkinson DA: Assessment of neurological dysfunction and recovery in alcoholics: CT scanning and other techniques. Subst Alcohol Actions Misuse 4:191–197, 1983

34. Cala LA: CT demonstrations of the early effects of alcohol on the brain, in Recent Developments in Alcoholism (Volume 3). Edited by Galanter M. New York, Plenum Press, 1985

35. Bergman H: Cognitive deficits and morphological cerebral changes in a random sample of social drinkers, in Recent Developments in Alcoholism (Volume 3). Edited by Galanter M. New York, Plenum Press, 1985

36. Freund G: Neurobiological relationships between aging and alcohol abuse, in Recent Developments in Alcoholism (Volume 3). Edited by Galanter M. New York, Plenum Press, 1985

37. Walker DW, Hunter BE, Abraham WC: Neuroanatomical and functional deficits subsequent to chronic ethanol administration in animals. Alcoholism: Clinical and Experimental Research 5: 267–282, 1981

38. Riley JN, Walker DW: Morphological alterations in hippocampus after long-term alcohol consumption in mice. Science 201:646–648, 1978

39. Walker DW, Barnes DE, Zornzetter SF, et al: Neuronal loss in hippocampus induced by prolonged ethanol consumption in rats. Science 209:711–713, 1980

40. McMullen PA, Saint-Cyr JA, Carlen, PL: Morphological alterations in rat CA1 hippocampal pyramidal cell dendrites resulting from chronic ethanol consumption and withdrawal. J Comp Neurol 225:111–118, 1984

41. American Psychiatric Association: Diagnostic and Statistical Manual of Mental Disorders (Third Edition). Washington, DC, American Psychiatric Association, 1980

4

Etiology and Neuropathology of Alcoholic Korsakoff's Syndrome: New Findings and Speculations

Nelson Butters, Ph.D.
David P. Salmon, Ph.D.

4

Etiology and Neuropathology of Alcoholic Korsakoff's Syndrome: New Findings and Speculations

Alcoholic Korsakoff's syndrome traditionally has been considered an acute disorder related to a deficiency in thiamine rather than to the neurotoxic effects of alcohol (1). According to this view, ethanol had no direct deleterious effect on the brain, and the average alcoholic did not have to be concerned with significant brain dysfunction from extensive alcohol intake if a normal nutritional status was maintained. However, a number of recent studies suggest that alcohol does have a toxic effect on critical cortical and subcortical brain structures regardless of the nutritional status of the organism. For example, Walker et al. (2, 3) demonstrated a significant reduction in hippocampal neurons, as well as a loss of dendritic spines on the remaining hippocampal pyramidal cells and dentate granule cells, in mice maintained for four months on an ethanol-containing but nutritionally balanced liquid diet.

Additional evidence for the neurotoxicity of ethanol emanates from numerous neuroradiological studies using computed tomog-

This chapter is an updated version of the presidential address delivered by Dr. Butters at the annual meeting of the International Neuropsychological Society, San Diego, February 1985.

Some of the research reported in this chapter was supported by funds from the Veterans Administration Medical Research Service, NIAAA Grant AA-00187 to Boston University, NINCDS Grant NS-16367 to Massachusetts General Hospital, and NIA Grant AG-05131 to the University of California, San Diego.

raphy (CT) scans (for reviews, see 4–6). Virtually all of these investigators reported that the scans of long-term, well-nourished alcoholics, as well as those of alcoholics with Korsakoff's syndrome, are characterized by enlarged cortical sulci and ventricles (including the third).

The results of these studies imply that the memory and cognitive disorders that characterize Korsakoff's syndrome do not appear acutely. Instead they seem to develop gradually over many years of alcohol abuse (the continuity hypothesis). As Ryback (7) suggested over a decade ago, there may be a continuum of cognitive impairment, the alcoholic Korsakoff patient being at one end of this spectrum and the heavy social drinker at the other. From this viewpoint, the conceptual, perceptual, and memory capacities of an alcoholic are functions of his or her drinking history (duration, quantity, frequency). This continuity notion does not deny the importance of nutritional factors; rather, it stresses the additive or interactive detrimental effects of malnutrition and ethanol abuse. As Freund (8) correctly noted, there is little evidence that chronic Korsakoff's syndrome ever occurs in malnourished individuals without a history of severe alcoholism.

The continuity hypothesis was the focus of two recent extensive reviews (9, 10) in which much evidence that the development of alcoholics' problem-solving, conceptual, and visuoperceptual deficits is consistent with the continuity notion is summarized. That is, cognitive functions dependent upon the integrity of association cortices seem to deteriorate as a function of ethanol abuse. In contrast, the severe anterograde and retrograde memory loss of alcoholic Korsakoff patients does not emerge slowly during years of alcoholism. Instead of a continuous deterioration, severe amnesic symptoms, which have been associated with damage to midline diencephalic structures (the dorsomedial nucleus of the thalamus, mammillary bodies) (1), emerge acutely with the onset of the Wernicke-Korsakoff syndrome. This dichotomy suggests that the conceptual, problem-solving, and memory deficits of the alcoholic Korsakoff patient may have distinct causes. The former may decline because of the direct neurotoxic effects of ethanol; the latter may be due to a distinct and acute neuropathological event.

In this chapter we update the previous reviews of the continuity hypothesis with new neuropathologic and etiologic findings regarding alcoholic Korsakoff's syndrome and speculate on the implications of these results for the neuropsychological profile of this disorder. To develop a behavioral background for this anatomical hypothesis, we first briefly review the major cognitive deficits of alcoholic Korsakoff patients and then discuss and update evidence (9, 10) of the limitations of the continuity hypothesis as an etiologic explanation of Korsakoff patients' amnesic syndrome. Following this discourse on the continuity hypothesis, we describe the findings of a recent neuropathologic study that serve as catalysts for speculation about the role of the basal forebrain in the memory impairments of alcoholic Korsakoff patients. Finally, some initial neuropsychologic data supportive of the anatomical notion being advanced are presented. We examine human and animal studies that demonstrate the importance of the basal forebrain structures in memory processes and compare the memory disorders of patients with alcoholic Korsakoff's syndrome, Alzheimer's disease, and Huntington's disease.

THE COGNITIVE DEFICITS OF ALCOHOLIC KORSAKOFF'S SYNDROME

The alcoholic Korsakoff patient's most striking neuropsychologic deficit is a severe anterograde amnesia. From the onset of illness, the patient is unable to learn new verbal and nonverbal information. Weeks or months of constant repetition may be required to learn simple things as doctors' and nurses' names or even the location of the hospital bed. This profound anterograde memory deficit is demonstrated experimentally as well by the severe difficulty in learning even short lists of five or six verbal paired associates (11, 12) and in retaining three words or consonants in working (short-term) memory for more than 9 sec if a demanding distractor activity intervenes between presentation and recall (13).

One of the most prominent features underlying the alcoholic Korsakoff patient's anterograde amnesia is an increased sensitivity to interference. A number of investigators showed that these patients are unable to acquire new information because of interference from previously learned material (proactive interference). These patients tend to perseverate responses (intralist intrusions) on short-term memory and free-recall tests (14, 15) and evidence improved learning and retention when learning conditions are structured to reduce proactive interference (13).

A temporally graded retrograde amnesia is also a distinct and consistent feature of alcoholic Korsakoff's syndrome. The Korsakoff patient is severely impaired in retrieving from long-term memory events that occurred in the 20-year period immediately preceding the illness. Surprisingly, remote events from the patient's distant past are relatively well recalled (16–20).

The sudden appearance of this amnesic syndrome in alcoholic patients has been attributed to the development of small hemorrhagic lesions in the dorsomedial nucleus region of the thalamus. In their postmortem study of 82 alcoholic Korsakoff brains, Victor et al. (1) carefully examined the medial diencephalic region in 43 cases. In 38 of the 43 brains, extensive atrophy of the dorsomedial nucleus was noted. Because the 5 brains without atrophy of the dorsomedial nucleus represented cases without lasting memory impairments, Victor et al. concluded that the dorsomedial nucleus of the thalamus is the critical structure for the amnesic syndrome. Reports of anterograde and retrograde memory deficits in patients with traumatic, vascular, or space-occupying lesions of the midline thalamus support the notion that the medial diencephalic region is instrumental in learning and memory (e.g. 21–25). Other investigators (for example, Weiskrantz [26]), convinced that the mammillary bodies must contribute to the amnesic syndrome, have stressed that Victor et al.'s findings can be interpreted as demonstrating that damage to both the dorsomedial nucleus of the thalamus and the mammillary bodies are precursory to the appearance of severe memory disorders.

Although the amnesic syndrome is the Korsakoff patient's most obvious cognitive deficit, impairments on visuoperceptual and problem-solving tasks should not be ignored. Despite attaining IQ scores well within the normal range, alcoholic Korsakoff patients are dramatically impaired on digit-symbol substitution tasks

(27–29), embedded figures tests (27–29), and various concept-formation tests that require the learning and shifting of problem-solving strategies (29, 30). Although there are some indications that these visuoperceptual and conceptual deficits, like the patient's memory disorders, may be due to damaged diencephalic structures surrounding the third ventricle (31), most investigators have attributed these disorders to some association cortex dysfunction (32, 33).

SIMILARITIES AND DIFFERENCES BETWEEN LONG-TERM ALCOHOLICS AND ALCOHOLICS WITH KORSAKOFF'S SYNDROME

Visuoperceptive and Problem-Solving Impairments

The most impressive evidence favoring Ryback's continuity hypothesis emanates from comparisons of the visuoperceptive and problem-solving deficits (cortical dysfunctions) of alcoholic Korsakoff patients and long-term alcoholics. For example, both alcoholic populations are consistently impaired on digit–symbol and symbol–digit substitution tasks. These deficits appear to be related to deficiencies in analyzing geometrical forms and to some retardation in learning specific digit-symbol associations (27, 28). For both Korsakoff patients and long-term alcoholics, degree of impairment on these substitution tasks correlates highly with their capacity to locate embedded figures and conduct a rapid visual search (28).

Although there are numerous demonstrations that detoxified long-term alcoholics are impaired on problem-solving tasks (for example, the Wisconsin Card Sorting Test and Reitan's Category Test (34–38)), only a few studies have directly compared the problem-solving strategies of alcoholic Korsakoff patients and long-term alcoholics with those of appropriate control populations. Oscar-Berman (30) administered a series of two-choice, visual discriminations to alcoholic Korsakoff patients, long-term alcoholics, patients with aphasic symptoms, and controls. This task, designed to evaluate hypothesis formation and focusing behavior, required subjects to discover the particular stimulus dimension (color, size, form, position) the examiner chose to reinforce. The results indicated that alcoholic Korsakoff patients could formulate and use hypotheses but their strategies were inefficient and insensitive to feedback provided by the examiner. The performance of the long-term alcoholics fell between those of the Korsakoff patients and the two control groups. Like the alcoholic Korsakoff patients, the long-term alcoholics did not fully use the examiner's feedback to guide their problem-solving strategies.

A recent study (39) confirmed these similarities in the problem-solving ability of alcoholic Korsakoff patients and long-term alcoholics. The task was a modification of the old parlor game "20 Questions" (40). Each subject was shown a presentation card with 42 stimuli (for example, outlined drawings of objects) arranged in a 6×7 matrix and was then asked to figure out which object the examiner was thinking of at that time. Subjects could ask any question as long as the examiner could answer yes or no. The subjects' goal was to identify the preselected object while asking as few questions as possible. Figure 1 shows the results for three trials of this identification task. Controls adopted the efficient strategy of first asking constraint-seeking questions, which reduced the number of possible alternatives (objects) by as much as 50%, regardless of a yes or no answer ("Is it a tool?"; "Is it in the first three columns?"). Only when two or three alternative objects remained did a nonalcoholic subject ask a hypothesis-scanning question, which referred to a single object ("Is it the saw?", "Is it the scissors?"). In contrast, both the alcoholic Korsakoff patients and the detoxified long-term alcoholics quickly abandoned this efficient use of constraint-seeking questions and shifted to hypothesis-scanning and even pseudoconstraint questions, which superficially seemed to be general in nature but actually referred to only one object on the card ("Is it something to tell time with?", which is only relevant to a drawing of a clock and not to any other alternative).

Two additional versions of the task were administered to the same alcoholic and nonalcoholic subjects. The first used 24 capital

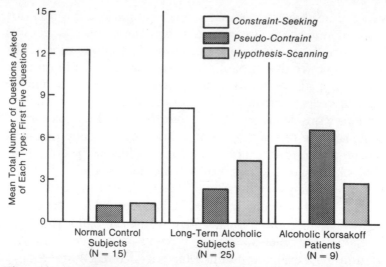

Figure 1. Performance of long-term alcoholics, alcoholic Korsakoff patients and nonalcoholic controls on Becker et al.'s (39) object identification task. Mean total number of constraint-seeking, pseudo-constraint, and hypothesis-scanning questions asked on the first five questions is shown.

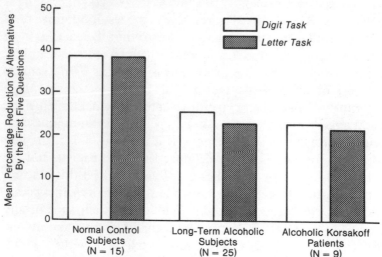

Figure 2. Performance of long-term alcoholics, alcoholic Korsakoff patients, and nonalcoholic controls on Becker et al.'s (39) letter and number identification tasks. Mean percentage of alternatives eliminated by the first five questions is shown.

letters (A–X), the second version, 24 numbers (1–24). The numbers and letters were arranged in 6 × 4 matrices and were printed on separate cards. The instructions and conditions for both tasks were essentially the same as those for the Object Identification Test, except that the examiner did not actually have a particular letter or number in mind. Despite this lack of a specified correct answer, the examiner provided feedback on the basis of the minimal number of alternatives eliminated by a yes or no answer. The subject was told yes only when that feedback eliminated fewer items than a no would have eliminated. This procedure prevented the subject from quickly guessing the correct item and ensured that at least five questions would be asked.

Figure 2 shows the results for three trials with the letter and number identification tasks. Nonalcoholic control subjects used efficient problem solving strategies, asking questions that eliminated almost 40% of the alternatives with the first five questions. Long-term alcoholics and alcoholics with Korsakoff's syndrome made much less efficient use of their questions, eliminating only between 20% and 25% of the alternatives with the first five questions. The two alcoholic groups' degree of impairment was virtually identical.

These findings, like those of Oscar-Berman (30), demonstrate that long-term alcoholics have not only a quantitatively significant impairment but also an approach to problem solving that is qualitatively similar to that of Korsakoff alcoholics. Both alcoholic groups seemed unable to initiate and maintain an optimal strategy for identifying the chosen objects, numbers, or letters. Such deficiencies in planning and problem solving have often been associated with damage to the frontal association cortex (41–44).

Two additional cognitive impairments that are often associated with damage to the frontal lobes are the ability to perform temporal order and event frequency judgments (45, 46). Because some studies (33, 47) suggested that alcoholic Korsakoff patients are impaired in such frequency and recency judgments, Salmon and Butters (48) examined whether non-Korsakoff, long-term alcoholics were also deficient in encoding these attributes of verbal and complex visual stimuli. An alcoholic group and a matched nonalcoholic control group were asked to remember two lists of words (or complex geometric figures) that were presented 5 min apart. Following the exposure of the second stimulus series, a recognition test composed of words (or complex geometric patterns) from the two presentation lists and an equal number of distractor stimuli was administered. For each test stimulus, the subject was asked to indicate whether it had appeared on one of the two presentation trials. When a subject correctly identified a word (or geometric form) as emanating from one of the two presentation series, he or she was then asked to indicate on which of the two lists the stimulus had appeared. The results from this test are presented in Figures 3 and 4. Although the detoxified alcoholics showed a mild deficit in identifying geometric patterns that had been presented previously, they were significantly impaired in judging the temporal recency of both words and geometric patterns they had correctly recognized.

The ability of alcoholics to perform frequency judgments was assessed in a second experiment. Detoxified alcoholics and nonalcoholic controls were asked to view and remember a 174-item (words, complex geometric patterns) list composed of 38 different stimuli. Six of the stimuli served as filler items, three at the beginning and three at the end of the list, to attenuate primacy and recency effects. The remaining 32 stimuli were target items and appeared in the list at one of eight frequencies (1, 2, 3, 4, 5, 7, 9, and 11 presentations). After the list was presented, the 32 target and 32 distractor stimuli were shown in a quasi-random order, and each subject was asked to indicate the number of times each item had been presented. If the word or geometric form had not been presented (that is, a distractor item), each subject was told to indicate a frequency of zero. The results of this experiment are presented in Figures 5 and 6. Although the alcoholics' judgments of frequency of occurrence were as accurate as those of the controls' when words were used, they demonstrated a significant deficit in judging the frequency with which geometric patterns were presented. Not surprisingly, the alcoholics' impairment was most apparent for geometric forms exposed 7, 9, and 11 times.

On the basis of these recent findings and the previously cited

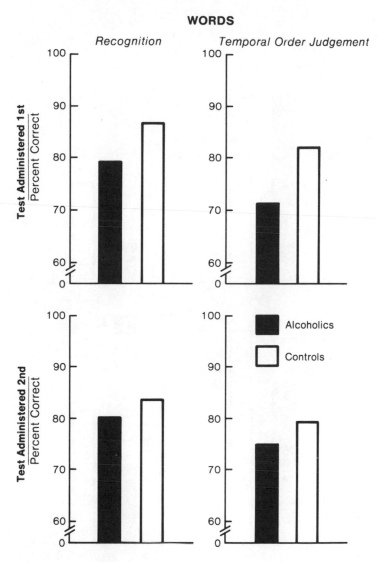

Figure 3. Performance of long-term alcoholics and nonalcoholic controls on the temporal order judgment task when words were used employed as stimuli. The mean percentage of correct recognition responses and correct temporal order judgments is shown. The results obtained when the word version of the task was administered before or after the figural version are presented in the upper and lower panels, respectively.

FIGURES

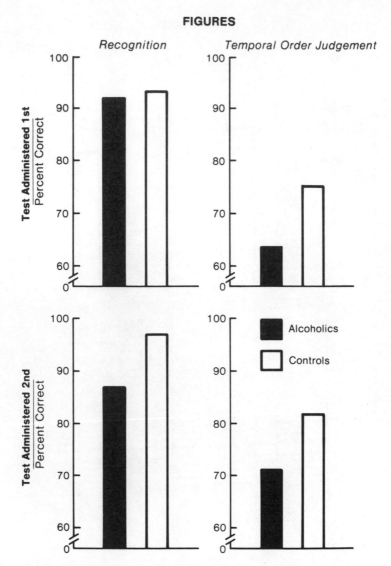

Figure 4. Performance of long-term alcoholics and nonalcoholic controls on the temporal order judgment task when complex geometric forms were used as stimuli. The mean percentage of correct recognition responses and correct temporal order judgments is shown. The results obtained when the figural version of the task was administered before or after the word version are presented in the upper and lower panels, respectively.

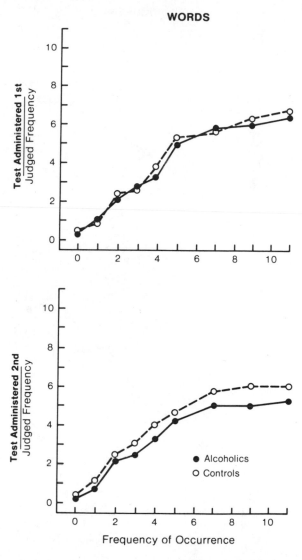

Figure 5. Performance of long-term alcoholics and nonalcoholic controls on the frequency judgment task when words were used as stimuli. The mean frequency judgments are shown as a function of the actual frequency of occurrence. The results obtained when the word version of the task was presented before or after the figural version are presented in the upper and lower panels, respectively.

FIGURES

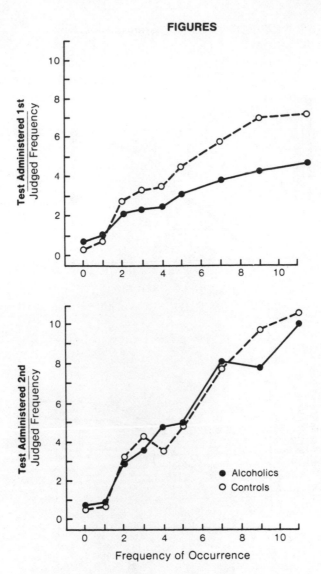

Figure 6. Performance of long-term alcoholics and nonalcoholic controls on the frequency judgment task when complex geometric forms were used as stimuli. The mean frequency judgments are shown as a function of the actual frequency of occurrence. The results obtained when the figural version of the task was administered before or after the word version are presented in the upper and lower panels, respectively.

literature on the problem-solving and visuoperceptual deficits of long-term alcoholics, it seems reasonable to conclude that the cortical dysfunctions of alcoholic Korsakoff patients may develop slowly during many years of alcohol abuse and do not appear suddenly with the onset of Wernicke's encephalopathy. The severity of the cortically mediated cognitive deficits evidenced by a given detoxified alcoholic may be more a function of how much, how often, and how long the alcoholic had abused alcohol than the development of an acute thiamine deficiency. This is not intended to deny that the chronic nutritional problems that plague many alcoholics may also contribute to the gradual development of their perceptual and conceptual problems, especially those apparent at the beginning of the detoxification period (49). We only wish to emphasize that the continuity hypothesis (7) seems to have its greatest applicability when one considers cognitive functions dependent upon the integrity of association cortex.

Memory Deficits

Unlike the cortically mediated cognitive functions, the available evidence concerning anterograde and retrograde memory deficits does not strongly support the continuity hypothesis. Although there are numerous demonstrations that non-Korsakoff alcoholics are significantly impaired on some memory tasks, these acquisition problems are quantitatively and qualitatively dissimilar to those of alcoholics with Korsakoff's syndrome. We review a few studies that demonstrate these differences and thereby question the applicability of the continuity model to the alcoholic's learning and retentive capacities.

Because of failures to demonstrate memory deficits in detoxified alcoholics with standard clinical tests such as the Wechsler Memory Scale, Ryan et al. (50) developed a battery of neuropsychological tests specifically designed to uncover subtle memory deficits. Among the tests used were a verbal paired-associate learning test, a symbol–digit paired-associate task, and a four-word short-term memory test with a distractor procedure (counting backwards) to prevent rehearsal. When Ryan et al. administered this battery of memory tests to alcoholic Korsakoff patients, thoroughly detoxified long-term alcoholics (at least 10-year histories of alcoholism), and age- and education-matched nonalcoholic controls, the two alcoholic groups demonstrated significant deficits on all memory tasks. The performance of the detoxified alcoholics fell between the scores of the normal controls and the amnesic Korsakoff patients.

In a second study, Ryan and Butters (11) again assessed the performance of alcoholic Korsakoff patients, long-term alcoholics, and nonalcoholic controls on the same battery of memory tasks. However, on this occasion the long-term alcoholics were divided into two subgroups: One group consisted of alcoholics who complained about deficiencies in their everyday memory; the other group was composed of alcoholics who claimed to have encountered no memory difficulties in their day-to-day existence. The findings of this study seemed to provide further evidence for Ryback's continuity hypothesis. The Korsakoff patients and the alcoholics with memory complaints were severely and equally impaired on all memory tasks. Although the alcoholics without memory complaints had significant deficits compared with nonalcoholic controls, their performance on the memory test was superior to those of the other two alcoholic groups. Unfortunately, the results of this study were flawed by the floor effects, which may have diminished significant differences between the Korsakoff patients and alcoholics with memory complaints, and by a failure to separate the nonalcoholic controls into two subgroups based upon their judgment of their memory capacities.

In a third investigation in this series (51) the memory capacities of young (mean age: 42 years) and old (mean age: 54 years) alcoholics with equivalant long-term drinking histories were compared. The results showed that both young and old alcoholics had poorer memory capacities than did nonalcoholics of the same age. More recently, Brandt et al. (52) replicated most of Ryan's results with a relatively large population of alcoholics ($N = 134$) and nonalcoholic controls ($N = 76$). Figure 7 shows Brandt et al.'s results for the symbol–digit paired-associate task. Although the difference between the alcoholics and their age-matched controls was statistically significant, the clinical relevance of the results is questionable. When alcoholic Korsakoff patients are administered this symbol–digit task, they average less than one correct response on each of the four learning trials. Thus, unlike the visuoperceptual and problem-solving tasks discussed previously, there is a vast difference in the severity of anterograde memory impairments demonstrated by alcoholic Korsakoff patients and long-term alcoholics. If, as suggested by the continuity hypothesis, the severity of the patients' memory disorders is a function of drinking history, these alcoholics, whose duration of alcohol abuse is similar (approximately 20 to 25 years) to that of Korsakoff patients, should have had more pronounced memory deficits.

Memory impairments in young and old alcoholics with matched drinking histories have also been reported by Becker and colleagues (53) on a paired-associate task that required subjects to associate 12 photographs of middle-aged men with 12 surnames (e.g., "Mr. Baker"). The alcoholics were significantly retarded in their acquisition of the face–name associations over nine learning

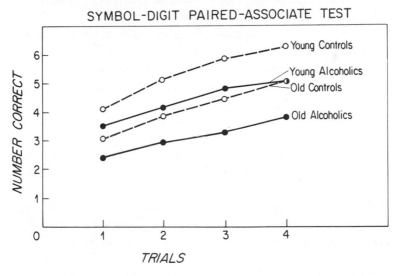

Figure 7. Learning curves of "young" and "old" alcoholics and nonalcoholics on the Symbol–Digit Paired-Associate Learning Test. (Reprinted from Brandt et al. [52] with permission.)

trials, but their learning impairment seemed mild when compared with the amnesic condition of Korsakoff patients. Because increased sensitivity to proactive interference is one of the most prominent features of the anterograde amnesia of alcoholic Korsakoff patients (for review, see Butters and Cermak [13]), Becker et al. (53) assessed the types of errors (omission errors, perseverative errors) produced by the two groups. No significant differences were found. This lack of evidence that the alcoholics' errors were related to an increased sensitivity to proactive interference provided no support for the contention that similar information-processing problems underlie the impairments of both Korsakoff and non-Korsakoff alcoholic patients.

Further evidence that increased sensitivity to proactive interference is not a major contributor to the moderate memory deficits of long-term alcoholics is found in their performance on the four-word short-term memory task developed by Ryan et al. (50, 52). On each trial of this task, the subjects are read four words and then asked to count backward from 100 by 3's (that is, a distractor task to prevent rehearsal) for 15 or 30 sec before attempting recall of the verbal stimuli. When alcoholic Korsakoff patients are evaluated on a simpler version (three words presented on each trial) of this short-term memory test, their severely impaired recall is usually characterized by numerous intralist intrusions. For example, if a Korsakoff patient correctly recalls "ship" as a word presented on the first trial of the test, he or she may recall this word on the second and third trials even though it has not been presented again. As seen in Figures 8 and 9, alcoholics are impaired on this four-word short-term memory task, but their errors are not perseverative (that is, intralist intrusions). Like nonalcoholic controls, alcoholics make primarily errors of omission.

When these findings are considered in conjunction with other data showing that alcoholic Korsakoff patients and long-term alcoholics have different patterns of encoding problems (54), little evidence supporting the continuity hypothesis can be found. Without some demonstrations that factors like increased sensitivity to proactive interference and deficiencies in encoding are as prominent in the retention difficulties of alcoholics as they are in

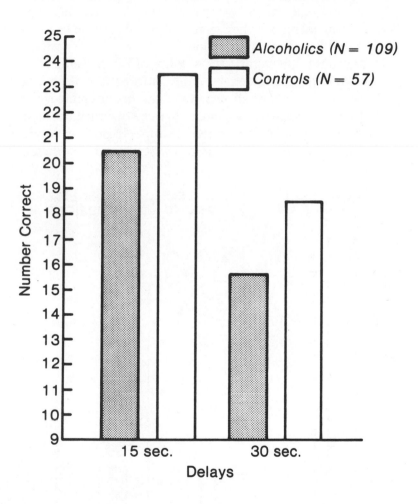

Figure 8. Performance of long-term alcoholics and nonalcoholic controls on Ryan et al.'s (50) four-word short-term memory test. Number of words correctly recalled after 15-sec and 30-sec delays is shown.

the anterograde amnesia of alcoholic Korsakoff patients, the alcoholics' moderately poor performances on short-term memory and paired-associate learning tasks remain ambiguous. If alcoholics and alcoholic Korsakoff patients are encountering problems with a given memory task for different underlying reasons, then it is difficult to maintain that they represent two points along a single continuum of cognitive dysfunction.

A third factor questioning the validity of the continuity hypothesis concerns the material-specific nature of the alcoholics' memory deficits. Almost all reviews of the neuropsychology of alcoholism have noted that alcoholics have more difficulty retaining patterned visual materials (for example, geometric forms, faces) than verbal information (for review, see 38 and 55), whereas

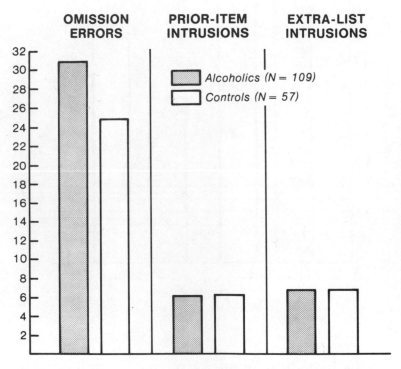

Figure 9. Types of errors made by long-term alcoholics and nonalcoholic controls on Ryan et al.'s (50) four-word short-term memory test.

alcoholic Korsakoff patients are severely impaired in acquiring both verbal and nonverbal materials regardless of the sensory modality used (13, 29). Our experiences with long-term alcoholics are consistent with this conclusion. Although we have found alcoholics to have significant and repeatable impairments on paired-associate tasks involving geometric patterns (52) and faces (53), deficits on verbal paired-associate tasks have been statistically marginal (11, 50, 51) and difficult to replicate. In a recent study with relevance to this issue, Becker and co-workers (56) assessed the performance of long-term alcoholics and nonalcoholic controls on three divided attention tasks requiring the retention of two series of stimuli simultaneously. One of the divided attention tasks used common words as the to-be-remembered stimuli, a second used single-digit numbers, and a third used photographs of faces. The results showed that only two of the three tests were influenced by long-term alcohol abuse. Both young and old alcoholics were impaired when faces had to be remembered, but neither group of alcoholics were impaired when words were used. On the numerical divided-attention task, only the old alcoholics encountered considerable difficulty.

Although we have focused our assessment on anterograde memory losses, a close scrutiny of the remote memory capacities of alcoholic patients also casts considerable doubt on the validity of the continuity hypothesis. As noted previously, the retrograde amnesia of alcoholic Korsakoff patients is characterized by a severe inability to recall major public and personal events for the 20- to 30-year period preceding the onset of the illness and by a temporal gradient in which memories from the patients' childhood and early adulthood are relatively spared. The results of the famous faces tests and the public events questionnaire used to assess the Korsakoff patient's retrograde amnesia in non-Korsakoff alcoholics provide little evidence of a remote memory deficit (57). This finding of intact remote memories in patients with 20-year histories of alcoholism suggests that the retrograde amnesia of the alcoholic Korsakoff patient cannot be attributed to a failure to learn new materials during their decades of alcohol abuse. Furthermore, the report (21) of an alcoholic Korsakoff patient's acute loss of the personal memories contained in his autobiography suggests that the ability to recall even emotionally pertinent episodes may be lost suddenly with the onset of the Wernicke-Korsakoff syndrome.

In conclusion, despite numerous demonstrations of anterograde memory problems in detoxified long-term alcoholics, Ryback's continuity hypothesis is difficult to defend for four reasons. First, long-term alcoholics with drinking histories similar to those of alcoholic Korsakoff patients have learning impairments that are far less severe than those of their amnesic counterparts. Second, there is little if any evidence that similar processes underlie the memory disorders of Korsakoff and alcoholic patients. Although the alcoholic Korsakoff patients' inability to acquire new information involves an increased sensitivity to interference, no evidence has been provided that the moderate learning deficits of alcoholics reflect this process. Third, whereas the anterograde amnesia of Korsakoff patients is not limited by modality or material, the alcoholics' memory deficits are most pronounced and reliable when visual patterned materials serve as the to-be-remembered stimuli. There is very little evidence that the typical long-term alcoholic has a consistent problem in learning and remembering verbal information. Finally, differences in the severity and nature of onset of remote memory impairments in alcoholics and in alcoholic Korsakoff patients do not suggest that retrograde amnesia develops slowly during decades of alcohol abuse.

ETIOLOGIC AND NEUROPATHOLOGIC CONSIDERATIONS IN ALCOHOLIC KORSAKOFF'S SYNDROME

Our review of the cognitive deficits of alcoholic Korsakoff patients and long-term alcoholics suggests that the continuity hypothesis has quite different merits when applied to cortical and subcortical dysfunctions. Visuoperceptual and problem-solving deficits, which presumably reflect the cortical abnormalities (for example, widening of cortical sulci) frequently seen on CT scans of Korsakoff and alcoholic patients (4, 58, 59), appear to develop slowly during the Korsakoff patients' 20- to 30-year history of alcohol abuse. Alcohol may have a direct neurotoxic effect on association cortex, and normal nutritional status may not protect the alcoholic patient from eventual visuoconceptual and analytical deficiencies. If Ryback's continuity model represents a good approximation of the relationship between alcohol abuse and higher cortical functions, then the daily consumption of a large quantity of alcohol for a sufficiently prolonged period may result in the "alcoholic dementia" described by Cutting (60) and Lishman (61).

When we examine the alcoholic Korsakoff patients' memory deficits, which have been associated with medial diencephalic lesions (1), the continuity model appears to have little applicability. Despite more than 20 years of severe alcoholism, non-Korsakoff alcoholics have relatively mild anterograde and retrograde memory deficits, which do not reflect the same information-processing impairments as those of alcoholic Korsakoff patients. The memory processes of alcoholics may evidence some moderate decline with continued alcohol abuse, but the truly amnesic performance of alcoholic Korsakoff patients cannot be achieved without some acute insult combining with the chronic detrimental effects of ethanol. Based upon all published clinical histories of this disorder, the most likely precipitating process is a severe thiamine deficiency (that is, malnutrition). The well-documented role of thiamine deficiency in the onset of the Wernicke-Korsakoff syndrome (see Victor et al. [1]) does not negate the possibility that the adverse effects of the combination of thiamine deficiency and alcoholism are exponentially worse than the effect of either factor alone. Freund's (8) conclusion that Wernicke's encephalopathy is followed by Korsakoff's syndrome only in alcoholics remains a clinically valid observation.

Given that the Korsakoff patients' amnesic syndrome does develop acutely because of the combination of thiamine deficiency and prolonged alcohol abuse, what neuropathological assumptions can be made? If one accepts the role of the mesial diencephalic region (especially the dorsomedial nucleus of the thalamus and the mammillary bodies) in the memory disorders of alcoholic Korsakoff patients (1), two conclusions follow. First, long-term alcoholism may result in minor damage to the medial diencephalic region, as evidenced by the findings of numerous neuroradiological studies. Some studies with CT scans have reported marked dilatation of the third ventricle in long-term alcoholics (for a review, see 4, 5, 62) whereas others using computerized analyses of the CT scans of alcoholics have reported that the density of brain tissue surrounding the third ventricle is highly correlated with performance on paired-associate learning tasks (63, 64). Second, severe thiamine deficiency is followed by a marked acceleration in the development of hemorrhagic lesions in the medial diencephalic region. The Korsakoff patient's precipitous decline in memory performance would then represent the exceeding of a critical threshold of diencephalic damage for the maintenance of relatively intact memory functions. The plethora of neuropsychological articles referring to alcoholic Korsakoff's syndrome as a "diencephalic amnesia" reflects the popularity of this neuropathological assumption (13, 65–68).

Despite the evidence linking Korsakoff's syndrome to the medial diencephalic region, Arendt et al.'s neuropathological investigation (69) suggests that the critical area affected in alcoholic Korsakoff patients may be the basal forebrain, the major source of cholinergic input to the cerebral cortex and hippocampus. These investigators, using cresyl violet stains and light microscopy, derived total neuron counts and indices of maximum neuronal population density in the three subdivisions of the basal forebrain and in portions of the globus pallidus. Of the 72 patients studied, 14 were controls, 3 were alcoholic Korsakoff patients, 5 were chronic alcoholics without dementia, 14 were Alzheimer's disease patients, 9 were Huntington's disease patients, and 3 were schizophrenics.

The major findings of Arendt et al.'s study are shown in Figure 10. In the Alzheimer's disease and Korsakoff's syndrome patients, the number of neurons in the basal forebrain was reduced by 70% and 47%, respectively. No significant loss of neurons in the basal forebrain was noted for the chronic alcoholics, schizophrenics, and patients with Huntington's disease. Of the five groups, only the Alzheimer's patients had a significant decrement (54%) in maximum population density in the basal forebrain. Scrutiny of the globus pallidus showed that only the brains of the patients who had Huntington's disease had significant reductions in total neurons (40%) and maximum population density (29%).

Although Arendt et al.'s (69) findings are based on a few brains and need to be confirmed by other laboratories, their implications for our understanding of the neuropathology and neuropsychology of Korsakoff's syndrome are obvious. From a neuropathological perspective, alcoholic Korsakoff's syndrome may be viewed as a cholinergic as well as a diencephalic amnesia. That is, the critical structures responsible for the Korsakoff patients' amnesic syndrome (and possibly other cognitive deficits as well) may lie both in the basal forebrain and in the medial diencephalon. The onset of severe thiamine deficiency combined with heavy alcohol consumption may result in the acute death of cells in the basal forebrain and, consequently, in a sudden and marked reduction of cholinergic input to those cortical and limbic structures involved with memory. If this is the case, hemorrhagic lesions in the diencephalon may be as common in long-term alcoholics as in

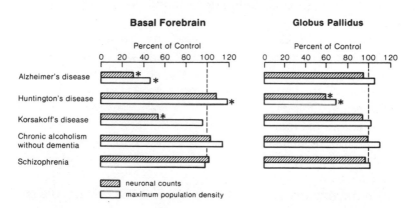

Figure 10. Neuronal counts and maximum population density in the basal forebrain and in the globus pallidus in five patient populations. Cell counts and maximum density for the five patient groups are expressed as a percent of such measures in 14 control brains. Bars with an asterisk indicate statistically significant deviations from the control indexes. (Modified from Arendt et al. [69].)

alcoholics with Korsakoff's syndrome and may be responsible only for many long-term alcoholics' mild-to-moderate memory deficits. This latter notion is supported by Harper's (70) neuropathological findings. Of 44 brains with indices (for example, hemorrhagic lesions, atrophy of the mammillary bodies) of Wernicke's encephalopathy, only 7 evidenced the classical clinical symptoms of the Wernicke-Korsakoff syndrome immediately prior to death. Apparently many alcoholics have a pattern of subcortical pathology similar to that of Korsakoff patients while manifesting only mild neurological and neuropsychological deficiencies.

This emphasis on the association between thiamine deficiency and the basal forebrain receives some indirect support from animal studies on the neuropathological effects of thiamine deficiency. As Irle and Markowitsch (71) noted in their careful review of this literature, there is little evidence that prolonged thiamine deficiency will result in consistent damage to the dorsomedial nucleus of the thalamus. Witt and Goldman-Rakic (72, 73) observed that multiple bouts of thiamine deficiency in monkeys were followed by lesions in the basal ganglia, cerebellum, and discrete brainstem nuclei. Most surprising, however, was the lack of necrosis in either the mammillary bodies or the dorsomedial nucleus of the thalamus.

Arendt et al.'s (69) failure to locate any cell loss in the basal forebrain of chronic alcoholics without dementia is consistent with our reservations concerning the application of Ryback's (7) continuity hypothesis to the memory disorders of alcoholics. Assuming that cholinergic activity is vital for processing and storing information, the intactness of the basal forebrain of chronic alcoholics without dementia makes it difficult to place long-term alcoholics and alcoholic Korsakoff patients on the same continuum of memory disorders.

It is important to stress that Arendt et al.'s (69) findings and our extrapolations to the Korsakoff patients' amnesic syndrome are not intended to deny the existence of diencephalic amnesia. There have been too many reports of amnesia following traumatic, vascular, and neoplastic lesions of the medial diencephalon to do so, although Markowitsch's (74) reluctance to attribute memory functions specifically to the dorsomedial nucleus of the thalamus should be heeded. In essence, our only goal is to establish a neuropathological basis for distinguishing the memory disorders of non-Korsakoff and Korsakoff alcoholics. The mild learning deficits of non-Korsakoff alcoholics may be due to damage to the diencephalon, whereas the severe amnesia of Korsakoff alcoholics may reflect the interaction of this diencephalic dysfunction combined with a large decrement in cholinergic innervation of the cerebral cortex.

RELATIONSHIP BETWEEN BASAL FOREBRAIN DAMAGE AND MEMORY DYSFUNCTIONS

Since the discovery of basal forebrain neuropathology in Alzheimer's disease (75, 76), there has been a growing interest in the functional role of the structures that comprise this brain region. As a result, a number of investigations of the behavioral changes that occur following relatively circumscribed lesions in the region, both in neurological patients and animal models, have been conducted. Because deficits in memory and its underlying processes are a hallmark of Alzheimer's disease, a preponderance of the studies have examined the relationship between basal forebain damage and memory disorders.

The importance of the basal forebrain structures in human memory processes has been demonstrated in a series of patients recently described by Damasio et al. (77). Five patients with basal forebrain damage were examined, including four with lesions secondary to rupture of anterior communicating artery aneurysms, and one with damage resulting from resection of an arteriovenous malformation. Intraoperative examination and CT scans revealed that, in all 5 cases, damage extended to a number of basal forebrain structures including the medial septal nuclei, the nucleus accumbans, the diagonal band nuclei, the medial portion of the substantia innominata, and the nucleus basalis of Meynert. Other brain areas often associated with memory, such as the medial temporal lobes and the midline thalamic nuclei, appeared intact. On clinical examination, the patients demonstrated a prominent amnesic syndrome involving both anterograde and retrograde amnesic symptoms. They were unable to properly integrate components of learned information (for example, the failure to associate a face and a name they could correctly recognize) and temporally categorize correctly recognized information (recency judgments). Damasio et al. concluded that the memory deficits resulting from lesions limited to the basal forebrain represented failures in retrieval processes. When the patients were provided with cues or administered recognition rather than recall tests, they achieved nearly normal performance on both anterograde and retrograde memory tests. Of course, on a behavioral basis, it is virtually impossible to differentiate between storage and retrieval deficits. Damasio et al.'s patients may have had mild to moderate storage problems, resulting in degraded engrams that were difficult to recall without extensive cues. The relative mildness of the noted memory disorders may have been due to the sparing of some of the structures comprising the basal forebrain.

Although further support for the importance of the basal forebrain structures in memory is provided by a number of animal studies, only a few of these investigations have used nonhuman primates whose brain organization provides a direct comparison with that of humans. In one report, Butters and Rosvold (78) compared the effects of ventral and dorsal septum lesions in monkeys on extinction of an operant bar press response. The ventral sector of the septum is of central concern because it contains virtually all of the medial septal nuclei, the basal forebrain structures that provide cholinergic input to the hippocampi and anterior association cortices. The results of this study showed that monkeys with lesions of the ventral septum were very resistant to extinction of a bar press response and made numerous repetitive (that is, perseverative) errors on a delayed-alternation task. This tendency to emit perseverative responses in quite disparate learning paradigms suggests that damage to the monkey's medial septal nuclei may lead to an impairment in associating responses with their consequences (that is, reinforcements). It should also be emphasized again at this point that both alcoholics with Korsakoff's syndrome and patients with Alzheimer's disease are well known for their tendency to make perseverative errors on both memory and problem-solving tasks (14, 15, 79, 80).

Additional evidence for a memory impairment following basal forebrain damage in monkeys is provided by Ainger and colleagues (81). Lesions of a portion of the monkey's basal forebrain (nucleus basalis of Meynert, or nbM) were produced by the injection of ibotenic acid. Although reductions of acetylcholine markers throughout the cortex resulted, the monkeys with lesions continued to perform as well as unoperated controls on a non-matching-to-sample task even when long sample lists (20 items) and substantial retention intervals (120 sec) were used. When scopolamine, an anticholinergic drug, was administered to the animals, a significantly greater memory deficit was observed in the monkeys with nbM lesions than in controls. Presumably, the lesions of the basal forebrain reduced cortical acetylcholine levels, but this loss was not sufficient to produce an obvious memory deficit. However, when challenged with scopolamine, levels of acetylcholine were lowered sufficiently to impair memory performance.

The basal forebrain of the rat contains some large, cholinesterase-reactive neurons known as the nucleus basalis magnocellularis. This area, believed to be homologous to the nucleus basalis of Meynert in human and nonhuman primates, appears to be the primary source of neocortical acetylcholine in the rat. Recent efforts at developing an animal model of Alzheimer's disease have focused on circumscribed lesions of this nucleus and any resultant memory deficits.

Lesions of the rat's magnocellularis forebrain nuclei (MFN) produce memory deficits in a passive avoidance task. In this paradigm, the animal is placed in a lighted compartment of a shuttlebox and allowed to step through a door into a dark compartment. Once fully inside the dark area, a shock is applied through the grid floor, and the animal is then removed from the apparatus for the duration of a retention interval. Following the delay period, the rat is returned to the lighted compartment, and its latency to reenter the dark area is recorded. The better the memory of the prior aversive event (the electric shock), the longer the rat will delay stepping through the door into the dark compartment. Using this passive-avoidance procedure, LoConte and colleagues (82) found that rats with ibotenic acid-produced lesions of the MFN were significantly faster than sham-operated controls in returning to the dark chamber of the shuttlebox following a 30-min delay.

Several subsequent studies have confirmed and extended these results. Flicker and associates (83) compared the effects of ventral and dorsal globus pallidus lesions in the rat. Lesions of the ventral region reduced indexes of acetylcholine activity (choline acetyltransferase, CAT) in the frontal cortex by 33%; no reduction was recorded after dorsal lesions. When memory was tested with the passive avoidance paradigm, only the rats with lesions of the ventral globus pallidus were impaired at delays of 1 and 24 hours.

Altman et al. (84) recently replicated these findings with 30-min and 24-hr retention intervals. In addition, they used a 5-min retention interval. Although impaired at the longer delays, the step through latencies of the rats with MFN lesions did not differ significantly from those of controls after the 5-min delay interval. This latter result is important because it demonstrates that the deficit observed at the longer delays is indeed due to a memory dysfunction. Other behavioral changes that could produce the same pattern of deficits, such as a tendency to perseverate or a lack of response inhibition, would be expected to occur equally at 5-min and longer retention intervals.

Deficits in T maze alternation tasks have also been noted following nucleus basalis magnocellularis (85) and medial septal nuclei (86, 87) lesions in rats. On this task, the rat must alternate between choosing the right and left arms of a T maze to receive food reinforcement. Thus, the rodent must remember its previous choice from trial to trial. Salamone et al. (85) found that rats with MFN lesions were impaired relative to controls in their alternation performance. Similarly, Thomas et al. (86) observed that preoperatively trained rats with medial septal nuclei lesions showed a deficit in alternation performance immediately following surgery. When these rats evidenced a slight but significant improvement over nine subsequent test (retraining) sessions, an approximately 100-sec delay was imposed between alternation trials. This additional retention interval resulted in a reduction in the operated animals' performance to chance levels.

A series of studies by Olton and his colleagues provide still further evidence for the important role of the basal forebrain nuclei in memory processes of rats. In the first investigation, Mitchell, and co-workers (88) reported that medial septal area (MSA) lesions resulted in significantly decreased theta activity in the hippocampus and entorhinal cortex of the rat. A significant decrease in acetylcholinesterase staining in these areas was also observed, and this decrement was correlated with the decrease in theta activity. Postoperatively, the rats were trained on a radial maze task in which they had to learn to retrieve food from the arms (8 or 12) of the maze in a nonrepetitive manner. Intact rats could readily learn to search for food only in arms they had not visited previously, but rats with MSA lesions (like rats with bilateral hippocampal lesions) were impaired in the learning of this orderly exploration of the maze.

A second study examined changes in sodium-dependent high-affinity choline uptake (SDHACU) in the rat frontal cortex and hippocampus following acquisition of the radial maze task (89). Because cholinergic afferents to the frontal cortex originate in the MFN, and hippocampal cholinergic afferents arise from the MSA, increased SDHACU in these areas reflect increased firing in the MFN and MSA, respectively. Wenk et al. found that the experience of acquiring the radial maze task increased the rat's SDHACU in the hippocampus, but not in the frontal cortex. This result suggests that the acquisition of some memory tasks may specifically involve increased activation of the MSA, and that the MSA and MFN cholinergic systems of the basal forebrain can be functionally differentiated.

From these findings with humans, nonhuman primates, and rats, it is evident that damage localized to the basal forebrain area is often followed by anterograde and retrograde memory deficits. These memory impairments appear to be mediated by decreased levels of cortical acetylcholine that occur as a consequence of the destruction of this subcortical brain region. In view of these demonstrations, the possibility that basal forebrain pathologic factors contribute to the alcoholic Korsakoff patients' memory disorders gains credibility.

NEUROPSYCHOLOGIC COMPARISONS OF ALCOHOLIC KORSAKOFF, ALZHEIMER'S, AND HUNTINGTON'S DISEASE PATIENTS

In addition to providing neuropathological data to account for the cognitive differences between alcoholic Korsakoff patients and long-term alcoholics, Arendt et al.'s (69) findings have substantial theoretical and heuristic value for neuropsychologists interested in cognitive similarities and differences among various demented and amnesic populations. If disruption of the cholinergic innervation of higher cortical areas is a common factor underlying Korsakoff's syndrome and Alzheimer's disease, these two disorders should evidence similar patterns of memory deficits. In contrast, patients with Huntington's disease whose neuropathology is known to initially involve the basal ganglia (90, 91) should perform quite differently from the other two patient groups. Because both Huntington's disease and Alzheimer's disease are progressive disorders in which memory deficits are often the first cognitive symptom (92–94), such group comparisons should be most productive when they involve patients in the earliest detectable stages of the diseases.

Although a number of studies have shown significant differences in the memory disorders of Korsakoff and Huntington's disease patients (for example, 21, 95, 96), only recently have such comparative investigations included Alzheimer's disease patients. Interestingly, the results of these initial neuropsychological comparisons are consistent with the expectations derived from Arendt et al.'s (69) neuropathology article. In a study concerned with the patients' pictorial memories, Huntington's disease patients, but not Alzheimer's disease and alcoholic Korsakoff patients, could use language to improve their picture-context recognition memory (97). Further, an analysis of the types of errors committed by three patient groups on the picture-context recognition task indicated that both the Alzheimer's disease and Korsakoff patients made many more perseveration (that is, intrusion) errors than did the Huntington's disease patients and intact control subjects.

Moss and colleagues (98) compared alcoholic Korsakoff, Alzheimer, and Huntington patients on a delayed nonmatching-to-sample task designed to assess recognition memory for different classes of stimulus material (verbal, spatial, colors, geometric patterns, and faces). For each type of stimulus material a recognition span was derived. The results showed that the Korsakoff and Alzheimer patients were equally impaired on each of the five stimulus conditions. However, the Huntington's disease patients, although impaired on four of the recognition conditions, were unimpaired in their recognition of verbal stimuli. When the subjects were asked to recall after a 15-sec delay the words used on the recognition test, the three patient groups were equally impaired. Martone et al. (99) also noted that Huntington patients, but not Korsakoff patients, can perform normally on verbal recognition tests and suggested that the verbal memory problems of the former group represent an inability to initiate retrieval processes.

In addition to these studies, some recently collected data in our laboratory on retrieval from semantic memory and the immediate recall of meaningful verbal passages also demonstrate similarities in the types of errors produced by alcoholic Korsakoff and Alzheimer patients. In one study, a letter fluency task developed by Benton (100) and colleagues (101) was administered to alcoholic Korsakoff, Huntington, and early Alzheimer patients and to groups of young (45 years old) and old (65 years old) normal control subjects. All subjects were read the letters F, A, and S successively and were asked to produce "all the words you can think of" that begin with these letters. The subjects were allowed 60 sec to generate words for each letter. Although this task has often been used to assess verbal fluency, Martin and Fedio (102) and Ober et al. (103) accurately observed that the test involves the retrieval of information from semantic memory (104). It has already been reported that patients in the early stages of Alzheimer's disease (102, 103, 105) and early and advanced Huntington patients (92, 106) are severely impaired on this letter and/or category fluency tasks, but direct comparisons of overall performance and error types among these two demented patient populations and patients with alcoholic Korsakoff's syndrome have not been attempted.

Figure 11 shows our findings for the letter (F, A, S) fluency test. The three patient groups all generated fewer total correct responses than did the two control groups; the performance of the Huntington patients was the poorest. The major difference in the performances of the three patient groups was seen in the number of perseverations produced on the test. A perseveration error is defined as the repetition of a correct word within a given category. For example, if a subject lists "fork" as the 3rd and 12th responses to the letter F, the latter response is counted as a perseveration error. To analyze the subjects' tendency to produce perseveration errors, the proportion of total responses that were perseverations was calculated. Although all three patient groups had a higher percentage of perseveration responses than did the two groups of control subjects (young = 1.9%; old = 2.4%), the alcoholic Korsakoff (11.3%) and Alzheimer (10.2%) patients had significantly higher percentages of perseverations than did the Huntington (5.8%) patients. As with the picture-context recognition task used by Butters et al. (97), the Korsakoff and Alzheimer patients, but not the Huntington patients, appeared highly sensitive to interference from previously emitted responses.

The investigation concerned with the recall of meaningful verbal passages also demonstrates that the alcoholic Korsakoff and early Alzheimer patients may be differentiated from the Huntington patients on the basis of their sensitivity to interference (Figure 12). In this study, subjects were read a series of four short stories similar to those used on the Logical Memories test of the Wechsler Memory Scale. Each paragraph consisted of 23 ideas or details concerning a specific incident. Thirty sec after each paragraph had been read aloud by the examiner, the subject was asked to recall as much of the information as possible. Although the alcoholic Korsakoff, Alzheimer, and Huntington patients were equally impaired in recalling the details, they differed in the number of intrusion errors. An intrusion error refers to the inclusion of an idea from a preceding story in the attempted recall of a subsequent

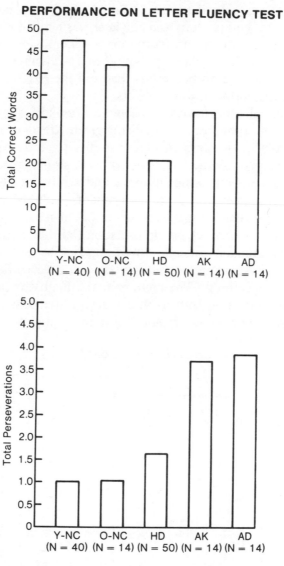

Figure 11. Performance of alcoholic Korsakoff (AK), Huntington's disease (HD), and Alzheimer's disease (AD) patients and of young (Y-NC) and old (O-NC) normal control subjects on a letter fluency task. Total number of correct words is shown on the top, and total number of perseveration errors is shown on the bottom.

passage. For example, if the idea "Tim had a brown dog" was mentioned in the first story read and later was recalled as an idea from the third story, an intrusion error was scored. As shown in Figure 12, both the alcoholic Korsakoff and Alzheimer patients made many more intrusion errors than did the Huntington patients and the normal control subjects.

These initial comparisons of alcoholic Korsakoff, Alzheimer, and Huntington patients are tantalizing given Arendt et al.'s (69) neuropathological findings. In all four studies, the early Alzheimer and alcoholic Korsakoff patients showed similar patterns of memory impairments, which in turn could be differentiated from the memory problems of Huntington patients. Although all three groups were severely impaired when asked to retrieve recently presented verbal materials and information from semantic memory, the Huntington patients proved superior to the alcoholic Korsakoff and Alzheimer patients on tests using recognition measures of verbal learning. Close attention to the qualitative nature of the patients' errors on both recall and recognition tests revealed that the alcoholic Korsakoff and Alzheimer patients are more

RECALL OF PASSAGES

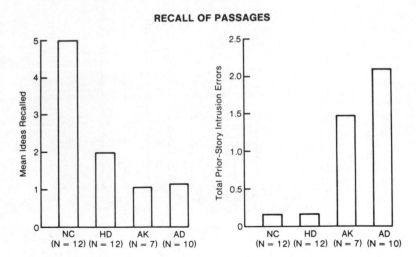

Figure 12. Performance of alcoholic Korsakoff (AK), Huntington's disease (HD), and Alzheimer's disease (AD) patients and normal controls (NC) on recall of short passages.

prone to perseveration and intrusion errors than are the Huntington patients.

Finally, it must be noted that this brief review of the comparisons of the memory deficits of alcoholic Korsakoff and Alzheimer patients has been at least partially a heuristic exercise. It is obvious to any student of dementia that there are as many differences between alcoholic Korsakoff and Alzheimer patients as there are similarities. Beyond the very early stages of their disorders, Alzheimer patients often develop dysnomia and severe constructional apraxia. In contrast, alcoholic Korsakoff patients show little evidence of a general language dysfunction, and their constructional difficulties are usually mild to moderate in severity. Even when we limit our comparisons to memory dysfunctions, there are indications that the previously described parallels may be misleading. For example, Weingartner et al. (47) suggested that although both alcoholic Korsakoff patients and patients with progressive degenerative dementia (probably Alzheimer's disease) are severely impaired in the acquisition of episodic memories (for example, learning a list of 12 unrelated words), the demented patients are more impaired than the Korsakoff patients in accessing and using previously acquired general knowledge (that is, semantic memory). This assumption concerning the intactness of the alcoholic Korsakoff patients' semantic memories can be questioned by their inability to recall overlearned remote public events (for example, the Watergate scandal). However, the clinical demonstration that alcoholic Korsakoff patients retain the rules of grammar and basic arithmetic is consistent with Weingartner et al.'s conclusion that semantic memory is more preserved in amnesic than in demented patients.

Given the convincing clinical and experimental evidence that alcoholic Korsakoff and Alzheimer patients are not identical in terms of their pattern of cognitive impairments, are additional comparative studies justified? In our opinion, there are at least two compelling reasons for an affirmative answer to this question. First, the noted differences between alcoholic Korsakoff and Alzheimer patients may represent differences in the amount of damage to the basal forebrain. If, as in Arendt et al.'s (69) study,

Alzheimer patients generally have more neuronal loss in the basal forebrain than do the Korsakoff patients, the additional disruption of language and constructional abilities in Alzheimer's disease may reflect a more drastic decrement of cholinergic innervation of the association cortices. If such is the case, further comparisons of alcoholic Korsakoff and Alzheimer patients in the earliest detectable stages of the disease would appear worthwhile. Second, comparative studies of various neurological populations have provided new insights into brain–behavior relationships. It was not long ago that all amnesic disorders, regardless of cause and lesion site, were considered a unitary dysfunction. However, because of the numerous neuropsychological investigations comparing the cognitive processes underlying the memory disorders of patients with diencephalic, hippocampal, basal ganglia, and cortical lesions, the heterogeneity of memory failures has come to be appreciated. Few would now deny that the anterograde and retrograde amnesias evidenced by alcoholic Korsakoff and Huntington patients involve different combinations of storage, retrieval, attentional, and motivational deficits. Such revelations should provide sufficient encouragement for the continuation of comparative studies aimed at uncovering the qualitative features of severe memory disorders.

CONCLUSIONS

We have attempted to emphasize the complexity of the etiologic and neuropathologic basis of alcoholic Korsakoff's syndrome and suggest some new directions in which to search. The continuity hypothesis, which derives support from the evidence that ethanol is neurotoxic, may be applicable to cortically mediated cognitive functions, but it seems inadequate in accounting for the severe anterograde and retrograde amnesic symptoms of Korsakoff patients. Although it is apparent that these amnesic problems develop acutely when severe malnutrition is combined with chronic alcoholism, the assumption that these memory dysfunctions can be attributed totally to hemorrhagic lesions of the medial diencephalic region can be questioned. On the basis of recent neuropathological evidence that alcoholic Korsakoff patients, like patients with Alzheimer's disease, have endured a significant loss of neurons in various structures comprising the basal forebrain, the possibility arises that alcoholic Korsakoff's syndrome might best be viewed as a basal forebrain as well as a diencephalic amnesia. The few neuropsychological studies in which the memory disorders of Alzheimer and Korsakoff patients have been compared provide some preliminary support to the notion that the memory disorders of these two patient populations have some common underlying features. Whether future neuropathological investigations of the brains of Korsakoff's syndrome and Alzheimer's disease patients do or do not confirm a common involvement of basal forebrain structures in these disorders, comparisons of the memory disorders of these and other neurological populations are still likely to produce new understandings of the processes underlying amnesic symptoms.

References

1. Victor M, Adams RD, Collins GH: The Wernicke-Korsakoff Syndrome. Philadelphia, F.A. Davis, 1971

2. Riley JN, Walker DW: Morphological alterations in hippocampus after long-term alcohol consumption in mice. Science 201:646–648, 1978

3. Walker DW, Hunter B, Wickliffe C, et al: Neuroanatomical and functional deficits subsequent to chronic ethanol administration in animals. Alcoholism: Clinical and Experimental Research 5:267–282, 1982

4. Wilkinson DA, Carlen PL: Chronic organic brain syndromes associated with alcoholism: neuropsychological and other aspects, in Research Advances in Alcohol and Drug Problems (Volume 6). Edited by Israel Y, Glaser F, Kalant H, et al. New York, Plenum Press, 1981

5. Wilkinson DA: Examination of alcoholics by computed tomographic (CT) scans: a critical review. Alcoholism: Clinical and Experimental Research 6:31-45, 1982

6. Wilkinson DA: CT changes and neuropsychological function, in Neuropsychology of Alcoholism: Implications for Diagnosis and Treatment. Edited by Parsons OA, Butters N, Nathan PE. New York, Guilford Press (in press)

7. Ryback R: The continuum and specificity of the effects of alcohol on memory: a review. Quarterly Journal of Studies on Alcoholism 32:995–1016, 1971

8. Freund G: Chronic central nervous system toxicity of alcohol. Annu Rev Pharmacol Toxical 13:217–227, 1973

9. Butters N: Alcoholic Korsakoff's syndrome: some unresolved issues concerning etiology, neuropathology and cognitive deficits. J Clin Exp Neuropsychol 7:181–210, 1985

10. Butters N, Brandt J: The continuity hypothesis: the relationship of long-term alcoholism to the Wernicke-Korsakoff syndrome, in Recent Developments in Alcoholism (Volume 3). Edited by Galanter M. New York, Plenum Press, 1985

11. Ryan C, Butters N: Further evidence for a continuum-of-impairment encompassing male alcoholic Korsakoff patients and chronic alcoholic men. Alcoholism: Clinical and Experimental Research 4:190–198, 1980.

12. Winocur G, Weiskrantz L: An investigation of paired-associate learning in amnesic patients. Neuropsychologia 14:97–110, 1976

13. Butters N, Cermak LS: Alcoholic Korsakoff's Syndrome: An Information Processing Approach to Amnesia. New York, Academic Press, 1980

14. Fuld PA: Storage, retention and retrieval in Korsakoff's syndrome. Neuropsychologia 14:225-236, 1976

15. Meudell PR, Butters N, Montgomery K: Role of rehearsal in the short-term memory performance of patients with Korsakoff's and Huntington's disease. Neuropsychologia 16:507–510, 1978

16. Albert MS, Butters N, Levin J: Temporal gradients in the retrograde amnesia of patients with alcoholic Korsakoff's disease. Arch Neurol 36:211–216, 1979.

17. Butters N, Albert MS: Processes underlying failures to recall remote events, in Human Memory and Amnesia. Edited by Cermak LS. Hillsdale, NJ, Erlbaum, 1982

18. Cohen NJ, Squire LR: Retrograde amnesia and remote memory impairment. Neuropsychologia 19:337–356, 1981

19. Meudell P, Northern B, Snowden JS, et al: Long-term memory for famous voices in amnesic and normal subjects. Neuropsychologia 18:133–139, 1980

20. Squire LR, Cohen NJ: Remote memory, retrograde amnesia, and the neuropsychology of memory, in Human Memory and Amnesia. Edited by Cermak LS. Hillsdale, NJ, Erlbaum, 1982

21. Butters N: Alcoholic Korsakoff syndrome: an update. Semin Neurol 4:226–244, 1984

22. Guberman A, Stuss D: The syndrome of bilateral paramedian thalamic infarction. Neurology 33:540–546, 1983

23. Speedie L, Heilman K: Amnesic disturbance following infarction of the left dorsomedial nucleus of the thalamus. Neuropsychologia 20:597–604, 1982

24. Squire LR, Moore RY: Dorsal thalamic lesion in a noted case of chronic memory dysfunction. Ann Neurol 6:503–506, 1979

25. Squire LR, Slater PC: Anterograde and retrograde memory impairment in chronic amnesia. Neuropsychologia 16:313–322, 1978

26. Weiskrantz L: On issues and theories of the human amnesic syndrome, in Memory Systems of the Brain. Edited by Weinberger N, McGaugh JL, Lynch G. New York, Guilford Press, 1985

27. Glosser G, Butters N, Kaplan E: Visuoperceptual processes in brain-damaged patients on the digit-symbol substitution tests. Int J Neurosci 7:59–66, 1977

28. Kapur N, Butters N: Visuoperceptive deficits in long-term alcoholics with Korsakoff's psychosis. J Stud Alcohol 38:2025–2035, 1977

29. Talland G: Deranged Memory. New York, Academic Press, 1965

30. Oscar-Berman M: Hypothesis testing and focusing behavior during concept formation by amnesic Korsakoff patients. Neuropsychologia 11:191–198, 1973

31. Jahro L: Korsakoff-like Amnesic Syndrome in Penetrating Brain Injury. Helsinki, Rehabilitation Institute for Brain Injured Veterans in Finland, 1973

32. Moscovitch M: Multiple dissociations of functions in amnesia, in Human Memory and Amnesia. Edited by Cermak LS. Hillsdale, NJ, Erlbaum, 1982

33. Squire LR: Comparisons between forms of amnesia: some deficits are unique to Korsakoff's syndrome. J Exp Psychol Learn Mem Cogn 8:560–571, 1982

34. Goldman MS: Cognitive impairment in chronic alcoholics. Am Psychol 38:1045–1054, 1983

35. Parsons OA: Brain damage in alcoholics: altered states of unconsciousness, in Alcohol Intoxication and Withdrawal (Volume 2). Edited by Gross M. New York, Plenum Press, 1975

36. Parsons OA, Leber WR: The relationship between cognitive dysfunction and brain damage in alcoholics: causal, interactive, or epiphenomenal? Alcoholism: Clinical and Experimental Research 5:326–343, 1981

37. Parsons OA, Farr SP: The neuropsychology of alcohol and drug abuse, in Handbook of Clinical Neuropsychology. Edited by Filskov SB, Boll TJ. New York, Wiley, 1981

38. Ryan C, Butters N: Cognitive deficits in alcoholics, in Biology of Alcoholism (Volume 7). Edited by Kissin B, Begleiter H. New York, Plenum Press, 1983

39. Becker J, Butters N, Rivoira P, et al: Asking the right questions: problem-solving skills in alcoholics and alcoholics with Korsakoff's syndrome. Alcoholism: Clinical and Experimental Research (in press)

40. Laine M, Butters N: A preliminary study of the problem-solving

strategies of detoxified long-term alcoholics. Drug Alcohol Depend 10:235–242, 1982

41. Damasio A: The frontal lobes, in Clinical Neuropsychology (Second Edition). Edited by Heilman K, Valenstein E. New York, University Press, 1985

42. Luria AR: Two kinds of motor perseveration in massive injury of the frontal lobes. Brain 88:1–10, 1966

43. Milner B: Some effects of frontal lobectomy in man, in The Frontal Granular Cortex and Behavior. Edited by Warren JM, Akert K. New York, McGraw-Hill, 1964

44. Stuss D, Benson DF: Neuropsychological studies of the frontal lobes. Psych Bull 95:3–28, 1984

45. Milner B: Interhemispheric differences in the localization of psychological processes in man. Br Med Bull 27:272–277, 1971

46. Smith ML, Milner B: Effects of focal brain lesions on sensitivity to frequency of occurrence. Soc Neurosci Abstracts 9:30, 1985

47. Weingartner H, Grafman J, Boutelle W, et al: Forms of memory failure. Science 221:380–382, 1983

48. Salmon DP, Butters N: Automatic memory processes in chronic alcoholics. Presented at the annual meeting of the Research Society on Alcoholism, Wild Dunes, SC, 1985

49. Albert MS, Butters N, Rogers S, et al: A preliminary report: nutritional levels and cognitive performance in chronic alcohol abusers. Drug Alcohol Depend 9:131–142, 1982

50. Ryan C, Butters N, Montgomery K, et al: Memory deficits in chronic alcoholics: continuities between the "intact" alcoholic and the alcoholic Korsakoff patient, in Biological Effects of Alcohol. Edited by Begleiter H. New York, Plenum Press, 1980

51. Ryan C, Butters N: Learning and memory impairments in young and old alcoholics: evidence for the premature-aging hypothesis. Alcoholism: Clinical and Experimental Research 4:288–293, 1980

52. Brandt J, Butters N, Ryan C, et al: Cognitive loss and recovery in long-term alcohol abusers. Arch Gen Psychiatry 40:435–442, 1983

53. Becker J, Butters N, Herman A, et al: A comparison of the effects of long-term alcohol abuse and aging on the performance of verbal and nonverbal divided attention tasks. Alcoholism: Clinical and Experimental Research 7:213–219, 1983

54. Cermak LS, Peck E: Continuum versus premature aging theories of chronic alcoholism. Alcoholism: Clinical and Experimental Research 6:89–95, 1982

55. Parsons OA, Prigatano GP: Memory functioning in alcoholics, in Alcohol and Human Memory. Edited by Birnbaum IM, Parker ES. Hillsdale, NJ, Erlbaum, 1977

56. Becker J, Butters N, Herman A, et al: Learning to associate names and faces: impaired acquisition on an ecologically relevant memory task. J Nerv Ment Dis 171:617–623, 1983

57. Albert MS, Butters N, Brandt J: Memory for remote events in alcoholics. J Stud Alcohol 41:1071–1081, 1980

58. Jernigan TL, Zatz LM, Ahumada AJ, et al: CT measures of cerebrospinal fluid volume in alcoholics and normal volunteers. Psychiatry Res 7:9–17, 1982

59. Ron M, Acker W, Lishman WA: Morphological abnormalities in the brains of chronic alcoholics. Acta Psychiatr Scand [Supplement]. 286:41–46, 1980

60. Cutting J: Relationship between Korsakoff's syndrome and alcoholic dementia. J Psychiatry 132:240–251, 1978

61. Lishman WA: Cerebral disorder in alcoholism: syndromes of impairment. Brain 104:1–20, 1981

62. Cala LA, Mastaglia FL: Computerized tomography in chronic alcoholics. Alcoholism: Clinical and Experimental Research 5:283–294, 1981

63. Gebhardt C, Naeser M, Butters N: Computerized measures of CT

scans of alcoholics: thalamic region related to memory. Alcohol 1:133-140, 1984

64. Jernigan TL: Computed tomographic findings in alcoholic vs. non-alcoholic dementia. Presented at the 10th annual meeting of the International Neuropsychological Society, Pittsburgh, PA, 1982

65. Huppert FA, Piercy M: Dissociation between learning and remembering in organic amnesia. Nature 275:317-318, 1978

66. Huppert FA, Piercy M: Normal and abnormal forgetting in organic amnesia: effect of locus of lesion. Cortex 15:385-390, 1979

67. Squire LR: Two forms of human amnesia: An analysis of forgetting. J Neurosci 1:635-640, 1981

68. Squire LR, Cohen NJ: Human memory and amnesia, in Neurobiology of Learning and Memory. Edited by Lynch G, McGaugh JL, Weinberger N. New York, Guilford Press, 1984

69. Arendt T, Bigl V, Arendt A, et al: Loss of neurons in the nucleus basalis of Meynert in Alzheimer's disease, paralysis agitans and Korsakoff's syndrome. Acta Neuropathol 61:101-108, 1983

70. Harper C: Wernicke's encephalopathy: a more common disease than realized. J Neurol Neurosurg Psychiatry 42:226-231, 1979

71. Irle E, Markowitsch HJ: Thiamine deficiency in the cat leads to severe learning deficits and to widespread neuroanatomical damage. Exp Brain Res 48:199-208, 1982

72. Witt ED, Goldman-Rakic PS: Intermittent thiamine deficiency in the rhesus monkey. I. Progression of neurological signs and neuroanatomical lesions. Ann Neurol 13:376-395, 1983

73. Witt ED, Goldman-Rakic PS: Intermittent thiamine deficiency in the rhesus monkey. II. Evidence for memory loss. Ann Neurol 13:396-401, 1983

74. Markowitsch HJ: Thalamic mediodorsal nucleus and memory: a critical evaluation of studies in animals and man. Neurosci and Biobehav Rev 6:351-380, 1982

75. Whitehouse PJ, Price DL, Clark AW, et al: Alzheimer's disease: evidence for selective loss of cholinergic neurons in the nucleus basalis. Ann Neurol 10:122–126, 1981

76. Whitehouse PJ, Price DL, Struble RG, et al: Alzheimer's disease and senile dementia: loss of neurons in the basal forebrain. Science 215:1237–1239, 1982

77. Damasio AR, Graff-Radford NR, Eslinger PJ, et al: Amnesia following basal forebrain lesions. Arch Neurol 42:263–271, 1985

78. Butters N, Rosvold HE: Effect of septal lesions on resistance to extinction and delayed alternation in monkeys. J Comp Physio Psychol 66:389–395, 1969

79. Fuld PA, Katzman R, Davies P, et al: Intrusions as a sign of Alzheimer dementia: chemical and pathological verification. Ann Neurol 11:155–159, 1982

80. Warrington EK, Weiskrantz L: An analysis of short-term and long-term memory defects in man, in The Physiological Basis of Memory. Edited by Deutsch JA. New York, Academic Press, 1973

81. Ainger T, Mitchell S, Aggleton J: Recognition deficit in monkeys following neurotoxic lesions of the basal forebrain. Soc Neurosci Abstract 10:386, 1984

82. LoConte G, Bartolini L, Casamenti F, et al: Lesions of cholinergic forebrain nuclei: changes in avoidance behavior and scopolamine actions. Pharm Biochem Beh 17:933–937, 1982

83. Flicker C, Dean RL, Watkins DL, et al: Behavioral and neurochemical effects following neurotoxic lesions of a major cholinergic input to the cerebral cortex in the rat. Pharm Biochem Beh 18:973–981, 1983

84. Altman JH, Crosland RD, Jenden DJ, et al: Further characterization of the nature of the behavioral and neurochemical effects of lesions to the nucleus basalis of Meynert in the rat. Neurobiol Aging 6:125–130, 1985

85. Salamone JD, Beart PM, Alpert JE, et al: Impairment in T-maze

reinforced alternation performance following nucleus basalis magnocellularis lesions in rats. Behav Brain Res 13:63–70, 1984

86. Thomas GJ, Brito GNO, Stein DP: Medial septal nucleus and delayed alternation in rats. Physiological Psychology 8:467–472, 1980

87. Rawlins JNP, Olton DS: The septo-hippocampal system and cognitive mapping. Behav Brain Res 5:331–358, 1982

88. Mitchell SJ, Rawlins JNP, Steward O, et al: Medial septal area lesions disrupt theta rhythm and cholinergic staining in medial entorhinal cortex and produce impaired radial arm maze behavior in rats. J Neurosci 2:292–302, 1982

89. Wenk G, Helper D, Olton D: Behavior alters the uptake of [^{3}H]choline into acetylcholinergic neurons of the nucleus basalis and medial septal area. Behav Brain Res 13:129–138, 1984

90. Kuhl D, Phelps M, Markham C, et al: Cerebral metabolism and atrophy in Huntington's disease determined by 18 FDG and computed tomographic scan. Ann Neurol 12:425–434, 1982

91. Sandberg P, Coyle J: Scientific approaches to Huntington's disease. Critical Reviews in Clinical Neurobiology 1:1–44, 1984

92. Butters N, Sax D, Montgomery K, et al: Comparisons of the neuropsychological deficits associated with early and advanced Huntington's disease. Arch Neurol 35:585–589, 1978

93. Josiassen RC, Curry LM, Mancall EL: Development of neuropsychological deficits in Huntington's disease. Arch Neurol 40:791–796, 1983

94. Miller E: Abnormal Aging: The Psychology of Senile and Presenile Dementia. London, Wiley, 1977

95. Oscar-Berman M, Zola-Morgan SM: Comparative neuropsychology and Korsakoff's syndrome. I. Spatial and visual reversal learning. Neuropsychologia 18:499–512, 1980

96. Oscar-Berman M, Zola-Morgan SM: Comparative neuropsychology and Korsakoff's syndrome. II. Two-choice visual discrimination learning. Neuropsychologia 18:513–525, 1980

97. Butters N, Albert M, Sax D, et al: Effect of verbal mediators on the pictorial memory of brain-damaged patients. Neuropsychologia 21:307–323, 1983

98. Moss M, Albert MS, Butters N, et al: Differential patterns of memory loss among patients with Alzheimer's disease, Huntington's disease and alcoholic Korsakoff's syndrome. Arch Neurol 43:239–246, 1986

99. Martone M, Butters N, Payne M, et al: Dissociations between skill learning and verbal recognition in amnesia and dementia. Arch Neurol 41:965–970, 1984

100. Benton AL: Differential behavioral effects in frontal lobe disease. Neuropsychologia 6:53–60, 1968

101. Borkowski JG, Benton AL, Spreen O: Word fluency and brain damage. Neuropsychologia 5:135–140, 1967

102. Martin A, Fedio P: Word production and comprehension in Alzheimer's disease: the breakdown of semantic knowledge. Brain Lang 19:124–141, 1983

103. Ober BA, Dronkers NF, Koss E, et al: Retrieval from semantic memory in Alzheimer-type dementia. J Clin Neuropsychol 8:75–92, 1986

104. Tulving E: Elements of Episodic Memory. New York, Oxford University Press, 1983

105. Rosen WG: Verbal fluency in aging and dementia. J Clin Neuropsychol 2:135–146, 1980

106. Butters N, Wolfe J, Granholm E: An assessment of verbal recall, recognition and fluency abilities in patients with Huntington's disease. Cortex 22:11–32, 1986

5

Prediction of Alcoholism Treatment Outcome: Multiple Assessment Domains

R. Dale Walker, M.D.
Dennis M. Donovan, Ph.D.
Daniel R. Kivlahan, Ph.D.
Douglas K. Roszell, M.D.

5

Prediction of Alcoholism Treatment Outcome: Multiple Assessment Domains

A major challenge in alcoholism treatment is defining an assessment process that predicts treatment outcome and improves upon treatment effectiveness by matching subtypes of patients to specific types of treatment. Although alcoholics share some characteristics and dynamics as a group, the research literature supports significant differences within the alcoholic population in regard to physiologic, psychologic, and sociocultural processes (1). These differences found within the alcoholic population argue against the idea of a single alcoholic personality and support subtypes of alcoholics. Proponents of alcoholic typology attempt to investigate subtypes more thoroughly by analyses of the alcoholic's preexisting biopsychosocial functioning and cognitive functioning before, during, and after drinking periods. Neuropsychologic deficits, for instance, have been associated with long-term abusive drinking and alcoholism (2–4). Impairment has been found in abstract reasoning ability, ability to use feedback in learning new concepts,

Presented in part at the annual meeting of the American Psychiatric Association, Dallas, May 1985. This research was supported by Merit Review Grant 338 from the Veterans Administration Health Services Research and Development Service and by National Institute on Alcoholism and Alcohol Abuse Grant AA04401. Data analysis was facilitated by funds from the Academic Support Services, University of Washington, Seattle, Washington.

attention and concentration span, cognitive flexibility, and subtle memory functions. These deficits have been assumed to impact the process of alcoholism rehabilitation and perhaps are useful in establishing prognosis in treatment.

A limited number of studies have begun to investigate the relationship between neuropsychological deficits and the treatment process. O'Leary et al. (5), for instance, found that the brain age quotient (BAQ) (6), an index of problem-solving and adaptive abilities, was related to clinical ratings of alcoholic patients' level of functioning on the treatment ward and to the likelihood of completing an inpatient treatment program. Parsons (7) also recently reported that the level of neuropsychologic function assessed at the fourth week of treatment was significantly related to clinicians' ratings of patients' interpersonal involvement and clinical improvement at the end of the nine-week program. Those patients who had been rated as having poor prognoses were found to have significantly greater deficits in abstracting, problem-solving, and perceptual-motor functions. However, the utility of the observed neuropsychologic test performance or the clinicians' ratings in predicting actual outcome is yet to be determined (7).

Inferences have been drawn concerning the anticipated effects of neuropsychologic deficits on the outcome of treatment. As Parsons (8) suggested, neuropsychologic deficits are usually associated with less effective adjustments to life tasks and demands. The alcoholic has a wide array of such demands upon the reentry into the posthospital environment. Tarter (9) and Chelune and Parker (2) suggested that the difficulties in abstracting and problem solving make it less likely that alcoholics successfully use those cognitive strategies in redirecting lifestyles and asserting control over drinking.

Results from recent research provide some support for these assumptions. Guthrie and Elliott (10), for example, found that impairment on a battery of tests assessing verbal learning, verbal memory, and visuospatial memory was related to lower abstinence rates and reduced after-care involvement at six-month follow-up. Other investigators (5, 11, 12) also found poorer drinking outcomes for more impaired patients. Gregson and Taylor's (12) findings further suggest that the level of impairment may be a more powerful predictor than measures of psychosocial or drinking-related variables.

It appears, then, that neuropsychologic deficits associated with alcoholism are prognostic of subsequent outcome. However, the amount of variance accounted for in posttreatment functioning by measures of impairment is relatively small (13). The question then remains concerning the centrality of neuropsychology in predicting treatment outcome. In this chapter we describe the shift in the thinking of our research group concerning this issue on the basis of a series of different approaches to information derived from a prospective treatment outcome study.

In 1979, our research group began a longitudinal, prospective study to investigate the interactive effects of neuropsychologic impairment and length of inpatient hospitalization on treatment outcome among male veteran alcoholics (14). The quality of neuropsychologic assessment for predicting treatment outcome was viewed as a central theme of the project. We hypothesized that the alcoholic group with a high degree of neuropsychologic impairment would have poorer treatment outcomes overall. Further, within this impaired group, it was expected that a poorer treatment outcome would follow a two-week hospitalization compared with a seven-week inpatient stay. Alternatively, when compared with the impaired group, patients with minimal or no neuropsychologic impairment were expected to have a better overall treatment outcome. The length of hospitalization for this unimpaired group was not expected to affect treatment outcome differentially.

METHODS

Subjects were male veterans solicited as volunteers from the Alcohol Dependence Treatment Program at the Seattle, Washington, Veterans Administration Medical Center. Patients were randomly assigned to either a two- or seven-week inpatient stay. A total of 245 subjects completed their assigned inpatient treatments and entered into after-care, consisting of once weekly group therapy meetings for a nine-month period. The sample was predominately Caucasian (90.3%), with small portions of black (7.3%), Hispanic (1.6%), and Native American (0.8%) patients. Most patients were from lower middle (42.9%) and lower (43.3%) social classes. The subjects averaged 45.7 years in age (standard deviation = 11.9) and 12.4 years of education (standard deviation = 2.8), with 76.6% having completed high school. At admission, 20% were single; 31.5% were married or remarried; 48.5% were divorced, separated, or widowed; and 52.3% reported cohabiting in a marital-like relationship within six months prior to admission. Also at admission, 20.8% of the subjects were employed full time, 36.7% were part-time or intermittently employed, 22% were unemployed, and 20.4% were retired or disabled. Average monthly income for the sample was $728 (standard deviation = $657).

Patients in this sample reported an average of 14.2 years (standard deviation = 10.6) of problem drinking, and 61.6% reported at least 10 years of problem drinking. Over half the sample (54.7%) reported five or more drinks per day for at least 45 of the 90 days prior to inpatient admission, with an average of 47.9 (standard deviation = 32.0) such heavy drinking days. The percentages of patients reporting positive alcohol dependence symptoms are as follows: loss of control after one or two drinks (82.6%), blackouts (81.4%), missed meals when drinking (78.5%), withdrawal shakes (77.3%), morning drinking (69%), and usually remaining intoxicated throughout each day (59.5%). Approximately two-thirds of the sample (62%) had previous alcoholism treatment and three-fourths (74%) had prior arrests related to driving while intoxicated. Thirty four percent of the subjects were court-referred for treatment.

The neuropsychologic status of patients selected for our investigation was established by Reitan's (6) BAQ, an age-adjusted index of current problem-solving abilities, previously found to discriminate between alcoholics and controls (15). The six measures that comprise the BAQ are the Category Test, Tactual Performance Test (TPT) total time, TPT Localization, Trail-Making Test (16), and the Digit Symbol and Block Design Scales from the Wechsler Adult Intelligence Scale (WAIS) (17). These are six of the eight

measures on which alcoholics have most consistently shown impairment when compared with controls (3, 4). The BAQ for each
subject was found by averaging T scores on all six of these tests and
then adjusting for age. For our research, the cutting scores for
establishing neuropsychologic groups was based upon trichotomi-
zation of the BAQ scores into high, middle, and low functioning.
Assessment of neuropsychologic functioning was made within
the first week of hospitalization (m = 6.3 days ± 3.2). Patients
reported an average of 23.7 days of sobriety (± 23.1) prior to the
first day of testing. Analyses indicated that neither length of
sobriety prior to assessment nor years of problem drinking were
related to the patient's performance on the BAQ tests (13). Subjects
were asked to complete structured interviews covering sociodemo-
graphic, occupational, drinking, and treatment-related information upon admission and at three-, six-, and nine-month postdis-
charge follow-ups. Such follow-up data were available for 192
(78.4%) of the initial sample of 245 patients at the nine-month
interval. Neuropsychologic data were gathered initially and at the
six-month follow-up interval, and data were available for 187
(76.3%) of the original sample.

RESULTS

Results are presented in four major sections and reflect the development of our thinking about assessment of the alcoholic and the
establishment of subtypes of alcoholics who might ultimately be
matched to more specific treatments.

Treatment Outcome: Neuropsychologic Status and Length of Inpatient Stay

There was evidence of significant improvement on all drinking
and nondrinking criteria for the sample as a whole. Table 1 reviews treatment outcome for the six subsamples from the experimental design (three BAQ groups by two length-of-stay conditions). Of the subjects for whom data were available, 44% reported
complete abstinence over the entire nine months after hospital

discharge. Information from at least one other source (spouse, friend, or therapist) corroborated this report.

The overall findings of the study (18) indicated that the length of time a person was hospitalized (two weeks or seven weeks) was unrelated to subsequent treatment outcome. Further, although neuropsychologic status was significantly related to treatment outcome, the relationship accounted for a very small portion of the variance in drinking status at follow-up. Those subjects with high neuropsychologic functioning, which is actually in the average range of the normative group, were significantly more likely to remain abstinent, have fulltime employment, and earn a higher average monthly income during the follow-up period. Therefore, treatment success, either continuous sobriety or a single isolated

Table 1. Treatment Outcome by Levels of Neuropsychologic Performance and Length of Hospital Stay

Performance	Two weeks (%)	Seven weeks (%)	Total
Abstinence (n = 192)			
Low NP	38.5	39.5	39.1
Middle NP	44.8	33.3	39.0
High NP	48.6	57.6	52.9
Total	44.4	43.6	44.0
Treatment success (n = 218)			
Low NP	30.3	45.2	38.7
Middle NP	56.3	34.3	44.8
High NP	53.8	51.4	52.6
Total	47.1	43.9	45.4
After-completion (n = 245)			
Low NP	22.2	43.2	33.7
Middle NP	38.5	22.0	30.0
High NP	46.5	40.5	43.5
Total	36.4	35.4	35.9
Full-time employment (n = 192)			
Low NP	22.2	34.2	29.2
Middle NP	41.4	30.0	35.6
High NP	57.1	57.6	57.4
Total	41.8	40.6	41.1

Note. NP = neuropsychological performance. Adapted from Walker et al. (18). Used with permission.

relapse over a nine-month period, could modestly be predicted by neuropsychologic assessment. Further investigation also suggested a potentially important interaction between neuropsychologic status and length of inpatient stay. Subjects with the greatest level of impairment were more likely to complete after-care and be employed full-time after a seven-week stay when compared with the two-week stay group.

After-care and Treatment Outcome

When accompanied by weekly outpatient after-care therapy, it appears that length of hospitalization may be shortened for many patients who seek alcoholism treatment without appreciably reducing treatment efficacy. Patients with reduced cognitive function, in contrast, may require a longer inpatient stay to perform more effectively in after-care. Perhaps, however, one of the more provocative findings in our investigations concerns the relationship of after-care involvement to all treatment outcome criteria except employment status. Of the total sample, 35.9% completed nine months of after-care. Chi-square analyses indicated a significant association between after-care completion and abstinence (χ^2 = 40.1, p < .001). The abstinence rate for those who completed after-care (70.2%) was significantly higher than for after-care dropouts (23.4%) (z = 6.36, p < .001). The dramatic difference in abstinence rates is consistent with findings of Costello (19) and Vannicelli (20). The opportunity for ongoing help and support for patients may be a principal advantage of after-care. Programs that emphasize relapse intervention may be particularly effective in maintaining after-care involvement and ultimate treatment success.

Neuropsychological Clusters: Subtyping the Alcoholic

The modest overall results found in relating neuropsychologic status to treatment outcome suggested a reexamination of the data to determine if other interactions were preventing a stronger predictive role. Donovan et al. (21) reevaluated the BAQ, the single summary score used to place subjects into the high-, medium-, and low-neuropsychologic status categories. Even though the BAQ had been validated previously (15, 18), potentially useful information may have been lost by summarizing six subscales into a total and including data from other neuropsychologic measures that were collected on this sample.

In order to investigate the hypothesis that distinct neuro-psychologic subtypes could be identified, the scores of 13 cognitive-neuropsychologic tests were subjected to an initial cluster analysis. The measures included the six components of the BAQ, the Group Embedded Figures Test, the Abstraction Score from the Shipley-Hartford Test, the TPT Memory Score, and the Arithmetic, Vocabulary, Picture Arrangement, and Picture Completion Tests from the WAIS. Using an average linkage clustering algorithm, 226 of the 245 original subjects were empirically assigned to three primary clusters or neuropsychologic subtypes of alcoholics.

Scores for the three alcoholic subtypes are found in Table 2. Subtype 1 has scores that fall into the average and unimpaired

Table 2. Means of Neuropsychological Tests Used in Cluster Analysis

Test	Cluster			Total sample (N = 226)
	1 (n = 95)	2 (n = 46)	3 (n = 85)	
Group Embedded Figures	11.4	7.5	3.4	7.7
WAIS arithmetic	11.1	12.3	8.9	10.4
WAIS vocabulary	12.2	12.6	11.0	11.8
WAIS digit symbol	10.3	9.1	7.1	8.9
WAIS picture completion	11.7	11.3	9.3	10.8
WAIS block design	12.1	10.8	7.6	10.0
WAIS picture arrangement	10.8	9.2	7.6	9.3
Category Test	34.6	45.4	75.4	51.9
TPT total time	10.8	17.7	24.1	17.3
TPT memory	8.4	7.2	6.9	7.6
TPT localization	5.7	2.5	2.8	3.9
Trail Making (Part B)	64.1	81.8	138.6	95.2
Shipley Abstraction	26.4	16.4	13.6	19.8

Note: All univariate F tests significant at $p < .00001$. WAIS = Wechsler Adult Intelligence Scale. TPT = Tactual Performance Test. Adapted from Donovan et al. (21). Used with permission.

range. At the opposite end, subtype 3 has below average and impaired cognitive and neuropsychologic functioning. Subtype 2 occupies a middle range on the continuum. Demographic evaluation of these subtypes showed that subtype 1 was significantly younger (mean age = 37.3 years) than the two other groups, which were of comparable age (mean age = 51.1 years). A difference was also found in the total years of problem drinking. Age and years of problem drinking may therefore produce a confound by interfering with performance within each subtype.

The most important criterion for validating these subtypes was their relationship to actual treatment outcome. In examining combined two- and seven-week treatment, there were no differences across subtypes with respect to abstinence over a nine-month follow-up. However, there was a difference within the seven-week program between the three subtypes. Subtype 3 (the most impaired) had the lowest abstinence rate (29.3%) even in contrast to the high rate (68.8%) of subtype 2, who were comparably aged. A significant difference was also found across subtypes with respect to the amount of time spent working during the last month of follow-up. This difference was maintained even when accounting for age and self-reported retirement or disability status prior to treatment. Subtype 3 was working the least. In summary, by investigating the pattern of performance on multiple cognitive-neuropsychologic measures, neuropsychologic factors were found to contribute considerably to treatment outcome, particularly in relation to employment.

Multiple Assessment Domains: Alcoholic Typologies

Although results from our previous research have reinforced the importance of neuropsychologic function in predicting treatment outcome, cognitive deficits appeared to represent only one of a number of other possible factors contributing to treatment outcome. Recently, Kivlahan et al. (22) and Meyer et al. (1) proposed a multiple-assessment domain approach to derive potential alcoholic subtypes. Typologies factors based on inclusion of measures from a broad range of variable classes might allow exploration of the development and maintenance of alcoholism. Further, more accurate treatment outcome prediction might be possible by developing such subgroupings.

In the most recent analysis of our data base (22, 23), three measures of demographics and social function, three measures of drinking behavior, two measures of neuropsychologic status, and five measures of personality derived from an abbreviated form of the Minnesota Multiphasic Personality Inventory (MMPI) were used. When the 13 variables were subjected to a sequential cluster analytic process, six subtypes were found. Table 3 shows the six subtypes and means on all the clustering variables. For convenience, subtypes are ordered by age from youngest (subtype 1) to oldest (subtype 6). However, age is not the only discriminating variable. Profiles reflect considerable differences on demographic, drinking behavior, neuropsychologic, and personality measures even when age is comparable, as in subtypes 4, 5, and 6.

Table 3. Means of the 13 Clustering Variables for the Six Empirically Derived K-Means Clusters

Variable	Subtypes					
	1	2	3	4	5	6
Age	31.3	39.1	42.2	49.9	54.2	54.7
Social Position Index[a]	58.5	59.7	58.1	50.8	46.0	61.3
Average hours worked per week[b]	29.2	12.5	9.9	20.2	12.9	14.2
Days of five or more drinks[b]	29.0	43.7	57.9	50.5	74.0	28.9
Chronicity (in years)	8.5	7.0	13.1	17.2	10.7	25.9
Alcohol Dependence Scale[c]	19.2	11.4	20.9	13.5	15.3	20.1
Brain age quotient	88.1	82.7	86.9	99.7	93.5	82.8
WAIS verbal IQ (prorated)	102.1	97.8	107.8	116.7	119.2	104.7
MMPI-168 depression	66.0	60.6	87.2	58.2	79.2	69.9
MMPI-168 psychopathic deviate	76.4	58.6	80.5	59.3	68.6	64.1
MMPI-168 psychasthenia	72.9	53.5	84.8	54.4	72.3	60.5
MMPI-168 schizophrenia	73.7	51.6	85.6	54.4	66.0	57.3
MMPI-168 social desirability	9.2	11.3	7.5	11.4	8.9	9.6

Note. WAIS = Wechsler Adult Intelligence Scale. MMPI = Minnesota Multiphasic Personality Inventory. Adapted from Donovan et al. (23). Used with permission.
[a] Hollingshead (25); lower values indicate higher social position.
[b] Based on the 90 days prior to admission.
[c] Skinner and Allen (26).

Instead of splitting a sample into a high, medium, and low neuropsychologic status, as done in our earlier research, these results revealed complex alcoholic subtypes that may characterize our clinical population more accurately than any single index score or subtypes based solely on measures from one domain (for example, neuropsychologic variables). Individual patients seen within our clinical setting seem to fit into the six derived subtypes. For instance, subjects in subtype 1 are relatively young, socially unstable, of average intelligence, but with subtle evidence of impaired problem-solving skills. Patients of this subtype have considerable psychological distress and alcohol dependence, despite a short period of problem drinking. Subjects in subtype 2 are also relatively young, but with evidence of marked neuropsychological impairment. Subjects have the shortest length of problem drinking and experience the lowest overall level of alcohol dependence. Similarly, these individuals show the lowest overall level of psychopathology. Both subtypes 1 and 2 experience the highest rates of after-care attrition in our program. However, they have an intermediate treatment success rate and are fairly likely to be employed full-time at follow-up.

Subtype 3 is composed of individuals of intermediate age and relatively low social position. Although the length of their problem drinking is at about the overall average for the entire patient sample, these subjects had been drinking heavily for nearly two-thirds of the pretreatment assessment period and also had the greatest level of alcohol dependence. They show the greatest level of psychopathology. Overall, they have the poorest treatment outcome and is the least likely to be employed full-time at follow-up.

Subtype 4 subjects have a relatively high social position with a good pretreatment work record. Although reporting a fairly lengthy history of problem drinking and consuming alcohol heavily on about two-thirds of the days prior to admission, this group has a relatively low level of alcohol dependence. They show the highest level of neuropsychologic functioning and little psychopathology. This group has the highest percentage of individuals employed full-time at follow-up and a high level of treatment success.

Subtype 5 patients, with the highest level of social position, are also among the oldest. Subjects in this group reported heavy drinking on more than 80% of the pretreatment days and had intermediate levels of drinking chronicity and alcohol dependence. However, there is a clinically significant level of depression and anxiety among group members. As a group, there appeared to be limited neuropsychologic impairment. Subtype 5 is the most likely to complete after-care, particularly if hospitalized for two weeks, and has the best treatment success rates.

Finally, subtype 6 has an age comparable to that of subtype 5; however, the former has a marked level of neuropsychologic impairment. It has the lowest social status, the most chronic history of problem drinking, and an extremely high level of alcohol dependence. Despite this, as a group it was drinking heavily for less than one-third of the pretreatment assessment period and show no significant levels of psychopathology.

It is of interest to note that within each subtype, there appears to be some differential effect of inpatient length of stay on treatment success. A longer stay (seven weeks) appeared to enhance outcome in subtypes 1, 3, and 6. Groups 2 and 4 appeared to benefit more with a shorter stay (two weeks). The remaining group (subtype 5) did comparably well regardless of length of stay.

The results of investigating treatment outcome in relation to subtype membership are presented in Table 4. For the sample as a whole, membership in a particular subtype was significantly related to after-care completion and employment status but not to treatment success. The same pattern was found for subtypes in the two-week but not the seven-week length-of-stay condition. There was a marginal difference across subtypes within the two-week length of stay condition with respect to treatment success.

These findings represent an initial step toward empirical subtyping of alcoholics by using multiple-assessment domains. Such efforts may lead to establishing prognosis and matching of alcoholic patients more closely to specific treatment modalities. For example, in Table 4, when treatment success is examined for subtype 1 patients, longer inpatient care was associated with better outcome, whereas a shorter length of stay appeared more effective for members of subgroup 4. These findings suggest that these derived subtypes reflect clinically meaningful typologic factors useful in predicting outcome.

SUMMARY

The present article provides a perspective on the role of neuropsychologic impairment in the prediction of treatment outcome among alcoholics. Although the observed cognitive deficits are predictive of posthospital function, particularly in the realm of employment, the role assumed by the level of neuropsychological impairment may be less central than has often been suggested. However, cognitive function measures can be incorporated with a broader array of variables derived from a comprehensive assessment process. Meyer et al. (1) suggested a number of possible variable classes to be included in the development of alcoholic subtypes based upon multiple assessment domains. These reflect the premorbid/demographic characteristics, pattern of alcohol use,

Table 4. Treatment Outcome of Subtypes by Length of Inpatient Stay (in percentage)

Outcome	Subtypes						Total	χ^2
	1	2	3	4	5	6		
After-care completion								
Two-week	5.9	29.4	30.0	46.4	69.2	40.0	36.4	14.9***
Seven-week	40.0	30.0	32.1	26.1	50.0	39.1	35.5	3.6**
Total	18.5	29.7	31.3	37.3	57.6	39.5	35.9	11.6**
Treatment success								
Two-week	29.4	52.9	20.0	57.1	53.8	35.7	42.2	9.5*
Seven-week	50.0	25.0	35.7	34.8	50.0	43.5	38.7	3.7
Total	37.0	37.8	29.2	47.1	51.5	40.5	40.3	5.4
Employment status (full-time)								
Two-week	55.6	35.7	13.3	70.8	38.5	10.0	41.2	31.2***
Seven-week	42.9	50.0	38.1	35.3	37.5	38.1	39.8	9.3
Total	50.0	43.3	27.8	56.1	37.9	29.0	40.4	24.2***

$*p < .10.$ $**p < .05.$ $***p < .01.$
Adapted from Donovan et al. (23). Used with permission.

degree of alcohol dependence, and pattern of both psychologic and physical alcohol-related consequences. Measures of important extratreatment factors, such as environmental stressors, coping responses, and social resources and supports, that have been shown to influence the recovery process (24) should also be considered.

Use of alcohol subtype methodology may prove useful in predicting prognosis and matching alcoholic patient subtypes to specific treatments. However, there are many unresolved methodological issues in developing these statistically derived typologies. Ultimately, the prognostic usefulness of alcoholic subtyping in the clinical setting will define its future directions in research.

References

1. Meyer RE, Babor TF, Mirkin PM: Typologies in alcoholism: an overview. Int J Addict 18:235–249, 1983

2. Chelune GJ, Parker JB: Neuropsychological deficits associated with chronic alcohol abuse. Clinical Psychology Review 1:181–195, 1981

3. Miller WR, Saucedo CF: Assessment of neuropsychological impairment and brain damage in problem drinkers, in Clinical Neuropsychology: Interface with Neurologic and Psychiatric Disorders. Edited by Golden CJ, Moses, JA Jr, Coffman JA, et al. New York, Grune & Stratton, 1983

4. Parsons OA, Farr SP: The neuropsychology of alcohol and drug use, in Handbook of Clinical Neuropsychology. Edited by Filskov S, Boll T. New York, Wiley-Interscience, 1981

5. O'Leary MR, Donovan DM: Cognitive impairment and treatment outcome with alcoholics: preliminary findings. J Clin Psychiatry 40:397–398, 1979

6. Reitan R: Behavioral manifestations of impaired brain function in aging. Presented at the annual meeting of the American Psychological Association, Montreal, Canada, August, 1973

7. Parsons OA: Do neuropsychological deficits predict alcoholics' treat-

ment course and posttreatment recovery? Presented at the Conference on Clinical Implications of Recent Neuropsychological Findings, Boston, MA, May, 1984

8. Parsons OA: Neuropsychological deficits in alcoholics: facts and fancies. Alcoholism: Clinical and Experimental Research 1:51–56, 1977

9. Tarter RE: Neuropsychological investigations of alcoholism, in Empirical Studies of Alcoholism. Edited by Goldstein G, Neuringer C. Cambridge, Balinger, 1976

10. Guthrie A, Elliott WA: The nature and reversibility of cerebral impairment in alcoholism: treatment implications. J Stud Alcohol 41:147–155, 1980

11. Berglund M, Leijonquist H, Horlen M: Prognostic significance and reversibility of cerebral dysfunction in alcoholics. J Stud Alcohol 38:1761–1770, 1977

12. Gregson RAM, Taylor GM: Prediction of relapse in men alcoholics. J Stud Alcohol 38:1749–1760, 1977

13. Donovan DM, Kivlahan DR, Walker RD: Clinical limitations of neuropsychological testing in predicting treatment outcome among alcoholics. Alcoholism: Clinical and Experimental Research 8:470–475, 1984

14. O'Leary MR, Donovan DM: Male alcoholics: treatment outcome as a function of length of treatment and level of current adaptive abilities. Evaluation and the Health Profession 2:373–384, 1979

15. Schau EJ, O'Leary MR: Adaptive abilities of hospitalized alcoholics and matched controls: the brain-age quotient. J Stud Alcohol 38:403–409, 1977

16. Reitan R, Davidson L: Clinical neuropsychology: current status and applications. New York, Halstead Press, 1974

17. Wechsler D: Wechsler Adult Intelligence Scale Manual. New York. Psychological Corporation, 1955

18. Walker RD, Donovan DM, Kivlahan DR, et al: Length of stay, neuropsychological performance, and aftercare: influences on alcohol treatment outcome. J Consult Clin Psychology 51:900–911, 1983

19. Costello R, Baillergeon J, Biever P, et al: Therapeutic community treatment for alcohol abusers: a one-year multivariate outcome evaluation. Int J Addict 14:215–232, 1980

20. Vannicelli M: Impact of aftercare in the treatment of alcoholics. A cross-lagged panel analysis. J Stud Alcohol 39:1875–1886, 1978

21. Donovan DM, Kivlahan DR, Walker RD, et al: Derivation and validation of neuropsychological clusters among male alcoholics. J Stud Alcohol 46:205–211, 1985

22. Kivlahan DR, Donovan DM, Walker RD: Alcoholic subtypes: validity of clusters based on multiple assessment domains. Presented at the annual meeting of the American Psychological Association, Anaheim, CA, August, 1983

23. Donovan DM, Kivlahan DR, Walker RD: Alcoholic subtypes based on multiple assessment domains: validation against treatment outcome, in Recent developments in alcoholism (Volume 4). Edited by Galanter M. New York, Plenum Press, 1986

24. Billings AG, Moos RH: Psychosocial processes of recovery among alcoholics and their families: implications for clinicians and program evaluators. Addict Behav 8:205–218, 1983

25. Hollingshead AB: Two factor index of social position. New Haven, CT, 1957

26. Skinner HA, Allen BA: Alcohol dependence syndrome: measurement and validation. J Abnorm Psychol 91: 199–209, 1982

Alcohol and the Brain: Some Problems of Interpretation

Donald W. Goodwin, M.D.

6

Alcohol and the Brain: Some Problems of Interpretation

It was the drinking I
did over the years that
wrecked half my brain.

—Norman Mailer (1)

The idea that alcohol causes brain damage is part of the common wisdom of our times. The Task Force for the *Diagnostic and Statistical Manual (third edition) (DSM–III;* American Psychiatric Association 1980) spent hours arguing whether there should be a category called "dementia associated with alcoholism" or "alcoholism associated with dementia." Apart from studies of the Wernicke-Korsakoff syndrome, there existed practically no evidence about which came first; the dementia or the alcoholism. Nevertheless, the committee opted for "dementia associated with alcoholism." The biases were too ingrained for any other decision.

In fact, alcoholic dementia is very rare, if the *DSM–III* definition of dementia is maintained. It is possible that no more alcoholics suffer DSM–III-dementia than nonalcoholics, that indeed dementia may lead to excessive drinking rather than vice versa. No one knows; the studies have not been done.

Not that alcohol effects on the brain have not been studied. Hundreds of articles and scores of books have been written on the subject. The literature is vast; the confusion just as vast. Hordes of decapitated rats have not cleared up the confusion. Generations of alcoholics in detoxification wards—captive audiences for generations of graduate students—have not produced a consensus.

The studies and reviews in this volume show that matters have not changed much since Wechsler observed the importance of distinguishing between the effects of acute alcohol intoxication and the long-term dysfunction ascribed to long-term continuous alcohol abuse (2)

Wechsler observed that studies of acute intoxication were superior to those of chronic effects because they could be conducted under controlled conditions. He concluded that acute and chronic studies were "mutually supportive, but whether they are interchangeable is open to question"—a classic example of fence straddling much emulated in the literature to follow.

From a methodologic standpoint, the studies in this book are greatly superior to many of their predecessors. One reason is that the investigators are highly sensitive to the complexities of the work they are engaged in: They hardly ever make a categorical statement without instantly qualifying or withdrawing it. This is all very healthy. The work will surely improve as a result.

The present commentary is devoted to some of the methodological and interpretive problems involved in brain-alcohol studies. Most have been touched upon by other authors in the book.

PROBLEM AREAS

Four questions arise in evaluating brain-alcohol research:

1. How does one explain the widely divergent test results?
2. To what extent are adverse effects from alcohol reversible over time and with abstinence?
3. Where there is evidence of intellectual impairment associated with alcoholism, which comes first: the alcoholism or the impairment?
4. Is alcoholism a unitary syndrome, or do subtypes exist with a lesser or greater propensity for intellectual impairment or brain damage?

Let us now deal with each area separately.

Divergent Results

The most consistent finding in the large neuropsychological literature on alcoholism is the observation that the IQ of alcoholics remains fairly stable regardless of how much alcohol they consume and for how long. Wechsler commented on this, and it has been confirmed by many other investigators, the most recent being Vaillant (3). In most studies, alcoholics do poorly on the Category Test of the Halstead Battery, the Wisconsin Card Sorting Test, and the Trial Making Part B test of the Halstead-Reitan Battery. Even in these tasks there are some contradictory findings, and in most psychological tests of alcoholics there seems to be more disagreement than agreement. Some possible explanations for the divergent findings are:

1. Sample differences.
2. Absence of control groups matched for age, race, education, and other demographic variables. Test results in most instances are influenced by age, and having even a few older alcoholics in the experimental group may skew the results.
3. Variable drinking histories. Presumably the duration and severity of the subjects' alcoholism are an important variable in test results, but these are often hard to ascertain. The onset of heavy drinking is particularly difficult to determine. The amount of drinking, which often changes from day to day, week to week, and year to year, is even harder to measure. Whenever a study refers to alcohol intake in terms of grams per period of time, the figure cited can probably be safely ignored on the grounds that drinking in real life can rarely be reduced to such precise quantities.
4. Time since last drinking bout and severity of bout. There is now ample evidence, as is discussed later, that test performance by alcoholics improves the longer they remain abstinent.
5. Nutritional status. Active and recently detoxified alcoholics are often malnourished. Vitamin deficiencies had been implicated in both the Wernicke-Korsakoff syndrome and alco-

holic peripheral neuropathy. Jernigan and associates' study in this book calls attention to the finding that alcoholics showing evidence of brain atrophy have the lowest body weight, suggesting they may be unusually malnourished (see Chapter 2 of this monograph). Dietary histories are as hard to obtain as drinking histories—perhaps harder—and the studies are really hard to fault on this ground, but nevertheless nutrition has to be considered.

6. Drugs. Many alcoholics, if not most, have used drugs other than alcohol, both before and at time of testing (psychotropic medication). Street drugs as well as prescription medication can adversely affect neuropsychologic performance.

7. Depression and anxiety. More than half of hospitalized alcoholics fulfill criteria for a major depressive disorder. Many are experiencing severe anxiety states. Both depression and anxiety influence scores on psychological measures (for example, depressed patients do poorly on the Category Test).

8. Motivation. This is an important variable in performing most tests. Recently hospitalized alcoholics, often heavily medicated and despondent about their situation, understandably would be less motivated to cooperate in testing than would individuals hospitalized for other reasons or healthy controls.

9. Beverage preference. Alcoholics rarely drink pure ethyl alcohol, but drink alcoholic beverages rich in congeners. These include the "higher" alcohols known to be particularly toxic. Whether some beverages are more harmful to cerebral function than others is not known, but the possibility must be considered.

10. Medical and neurologic illnesses associated with alcoholism. Not only are alcoholics often malnourished and have liver disease, they are almost universally heavy smokers, are frequently subject to head trauma, and differ from other groups in their habits and lifestyles. All of these factors may influence test results.

11. Volunteer status. Cox and Sipprelle (4) found that volunteer-nonvolunteer status was an important variable in determin-

ing the results of a heart-rate conditioning experiment. If a conditioning experiment can be thus influenced, the importance of motivation in taking a battery of psychological tests is obvious.

Reversibility

Studies in recent years have repeatedly shown that alcoholics progressively improve in psychological test performance the longer they remain abstinent. As ably reviewed by Grant et al. in Chapter 3 of this monograph, the recoverability rate in alcoholics is difficult to determine because of highly diverse reports in the literature. Some follow-up studies report essentially no improvement in test performance, others report some improvement, and still others report total restoration to normal, particularly in alcoholics who have abstained for many months or years. As the authors indicate, "alcoholics who are able to maintain stable abstinence for long periods of time can have neuropsychological performances which are essentially normal" (p. 70). In thus summarizing the diverse findings, Grant et al. point out that a certain number of alcoholics may experience a subacute, subtle, stable, cognitive deficit which, "while not interfering with ordinary functioning, might nevertheless indicate a persisting organic mental disorder" (p. 79). Their main emphasis, however, is on the impressive literature suggesting that large number of alcoholics return to normal functioning after long periods of abstinence or near abstinence, and they cite a number of studies to support this contention. Because the observation about reversibility is so important (and may even have prognostic implications for treatment, as Walker et al. report in Chapter 5 of this monograph), I cite a few studies not mentioned in the otherwise comprehensive review by Grant, Adams, and Reed.

1.   White (5) administered an object-sorting test to a group of 50 Alcoholics Anonymous members and found that those sober from one to three months made significantly less "abstract-volitional shifts" than those with three years of sobriety.
2.   In a study by Jonsson et al. (6), in which a large number of

intellectual function tests were administered to alcoholics, it was found that performances were worse in the group that was examined at the beginning of the term in hospital than in the group examined at the end. In only two tests—Wechsler's Digit Symbol and Grassi's Block Substitution Test—was there no evidence of restitution by the end of hospitalization. On this basis one might presume that the general trend implies a partially reversible impairment of intellectual ability immediately following a period of intensive alcohol abuse.

3. Plumeau et al. (7) compared alcoholics in remission (at least two years' abstinent) with unremitted alcoholics and found the latter group had poorer test results than controls and the remitted cases. Both alcoholic groups were identical as regard to the duration and intensity of alcoholism. An analysis of Wechsler Adult Intelligence Scale (WAIS) subscales revealed no differences between the remitted alcoholics and normal controls.

4. Smith and Layden (8) showed improvement in perceptual motor function after prolonged abstinence from alcohol, comparing alcoholics during and after hospital treatment.

5. Goldstein (9) showed that gait instability in alcoholics is reversible and practice potentiates the degree of improvement.

6. Smith et al. (10) administered tests to alcoholics soon after admission and again after two weeks. Significant improvement was found on the second testing with regard to Shipley-Hartford measures of vocabulary and abstract reasoning, the Embedded Figures Test, and the Hidden Figures Test.

7. Weingartner et al. (11) and Allen et al. (12) demonstrated a postbinge syndrome, which included a learning deficit attributable to an impairment in holding information in memory or storage. This Korsakoff-like deficit disappeared after three weeks of abstinence in the hospital.

8. Witkin et al. (13) reported that alcoholics were more "field dependent" than nonalcoholics, but Goldstein and Chotlos (14) reported they became more field independent after a period of abstinence.

9. In a study by Goodwin and Hill (unpublished data), it was

found that 8 of 16 newly admitted alcoholics manifested "organicity" on a test developed by Canter based on a modification of the Bender Gestalt Test. The test involves redrawing the Bender designs on paper that has a light background of wavy lines. In patients with brain damage, this background apparently "interferes" with the ability to reproduce the Bender design and the test has been called the Background Interference Procedure (BIP). Although the test has been well validated as a measure of chronic brain damage, it was found the "brain-damaged" alcoholics improved significantly in their performance on the test after one month in the hospital.

These examples illustrate the importance of separating acute from chronic effects of alcohol and the difficulties in doing this by studying recently hospitalized patients. The evidence is strong that at least some of the deficits from abuse of alcohol are indeed reversible, including deficits in abstracting ability.

How might one explain the reversibility? One explanation has been that alcoholics improve over time in taking psychological tests because they take the same tests over and over and therefore benefit from practice. Grant et al. point out in Chapter 3 of this monograph that this may be a partial explanation but that alcoholics who have never had a particular test before but have been abstinent for several weeks will perform better than alcoholics tested in the first week, suggesting that improvement is not simply due to practice.

Reversibility is not limited to neuropsychologic testing. Of the many computed tomography (CT) studies of alcoholics, most show sulcal widening and ventricular dilatation, but two studies (15, 16) show a trend toward normalization of brain structure after alcoholics stop drinking for varying periods of time. In Chapter 2 of this monograph, Jernigan et al. describe their finding that widening occurred in alcoholics of all ages, but ventricular dilitation was more or less limited to alcoholics over the age of 40 years. In other words, signs of atrophy were not correlated in all instances with duration and extent of drinking (nor, in some studies, with clinical condition or psychological tests performance).

Given that brain cells do not grow back, how does one explain the reversibility of what appears to be atrophy? One explanation is that with sobriety, the alcoholics' dendrites proliferate. Another explanation is that sulcal widening and ventricular dilatation are due to fluid shifts (Maurice Victor, personal communication, April 14, 1985). Both explanations sound reasonable and are not mutually incompatible. Alcoholics, when they are drinking and for a period afterward, are overhydrated, and brain water in chronic alcoholic patients as measured by magnetic resonance imaging is increased (17). (The old term *wet brain* may indeed be apt).

Therefore, whether neuronal loss is the basis for CT evidence of atrophy remains uncertain. Animal studies have been of little help. Some studies (18) show that rats exposed to months of alcohol exposure lose brain cells, but other studies (19) show no loss. Reduced dendrites have been reported in alcohol-fed rats, which supports the hypothesis that reversal of CT abnormalities may be due to dendritic proliferation (19).

Cart or Horse?

A major problem in concluding that alcohol causes cognitive deficits and brain atrophy is that rarely is there any information about the subjects' cognitive or brain status before they began drinking. It is possible that those subjects who show impairment would have shown impairment had they been teetotalers. Kaij, in his classical twin study (20), reported a finding that illustrates the difficulty in evaluating chronic effects of alcohol on intellectual functioning and the possibility that what is often interpreted as consequence is, on the contrary, cause.

Kaij administered a series of cognitive tests to twin pairs where one of the twins was alcoholic. He found that "deterioration" was more correlated with zygosity than with extent of drinking. That is, a "deteriorated" heavy drinking monozygotic twin was more likely to have a light drinking partner showing signs of deterioration than was true of dyzygotic twins where one partner was deteriorated. He interpreted this as indicating that so-called "alcoholic deterioration" occurred more or less independently of alcohol consumption and may be a genetically determined contributor to the illness rather than a consequence.

Longitudinal studies would be useful in determining whether cognitive deficits preceded as well as followed alcohol consumption. However, there are not many such studies. The ones that exist used cohorts studied in adolescence, many years before the follow-up and before the kinds of tests that might be useful in predicting future alcoholism existed or were thought to be important.

One alternative approach to distinguishing cause from consequence is to study children of alcoholics before they begin drinking (called "high-risk" studies, because about 1 of 4 sons themselves become alcoholic). Some neuropsychologic studies of the children of alcoholics report intellectual deficits, but others do not. A recent study in Denmark (21) found that late-adolescent sons of alcoholics performed less well on the Category Test of the Halstead battery than did controls without alcoholism in their parentage. This was interesting because, of all the tests administered to alcoholics, the Category Test most frequently shows impairment, and this is usually attributed to selective effects of drinking on "abstracting ability" or "conceptual shifting." However, if children of alcoholics have problems with the Category Test even before they start drinking, what was interpreted as a consequence of drinking may indeed have no relevance to drinking, or might even have a causal role.

The same possibility applies to CT abnormalities found in alcoholics. The abnormalities may have preceded the drinking. Longitudinal studies do not exist to provide an answer, but studies of the children of alcoholics again suggest that anatomical abnormalities occur more frequently in children of alcoholics than in controls; therefore, there might be a causal relationship to the development of alcoholism (22). Similarly, Event-Related-Potentials (ERPs) recorded on the electroencephalogram (EEG) show abnormalities in both alcoholics and their nonalcoholic children, posing once again the possibility that a presumed consequence of drinking may indeed be a cause (22).

Are Alcoholics All the Same?

Almost everyone agrees that alcoholics are not the same, but there is little agreement about how to subdivide alcoholism into subtypes. *DSM–III*, for example, categorizes patients who formerly were called alcoholics into alcohol abusers and alcohol-dependent individuals (a distinction that will probably be dropped in future editions).

One of the more promising subtypes to emerge in recent years is the distinction between familial and nonfamilial alcoholism. Familial alcoholism has an earlier onset and a more severe course and may be more resistant to treatment. Oscar Parsons and colleagues reported that a family history of alcoholism predicts performance on psychological tests (23). For example, nonalcoholics lacking a family history of alcoholism did well on psychological tests. Alcoholics with a family history of alcoholism did poorly. Alternatively, nonalcoholics and alcoholics had rather similar test scores if the nonalcoholics had a family history of alcoholism and the alcoholics did not. To emphasize the complexity of the area, recent data from Grant et al. failed to reveal an association between neuropsychological performance and family history in groups of alcoholics varying in the strength of the first-degree family history of alcoholism (24). Porjesz and Begleiter (22) found that family history predicts structural brain changes: alcoholics with a positive family history have larger ventricles and abnormal P300s on the EEG than those without a family history of alcoholism. Finally, alcoholics with a family history of alcoholism more have been noted more often to be hyperactive as children than were nonfamilial alcoholics (25).

CONCLUSION

In summary, alcoholism unquestionably is associated with brain damage, Korsakoff's syndrome being the classic example. Its association with permanently impaired intellectual functioning is more equivocal, principally because of the relatively few studies of alcoholics who have stopped drinking for long periods of time and the likely confusion of acute with chronic effects. Moreover, to the extent it exists, the association is with alcoholism rather than with alcohol.

Alcoholism is a clinical syndrome characterized not only by excessive consumption of alcohol but also by malnutrition, a high incidence of head trauma, heavy smoking, liver disease, other medical complications, and usually, a highly irregular lifestyle. Some indirect evidence (24) does suggest that alcohol may have a permanent effect on brain function, but this evidence is based on anatomical and biochemical data more so than clinical observation or psychological tests.

Indeed, it is impressive how well alcoholics perform on psychological tests, given all of the potentially harmful influences noted previously. Even after many years of very heavy drinking, alcoholics show little objective evidence of brain damage provided a sufficiently long period has passed between the last drink and time of testing. It is generally believed (see Chapter 3) that residual effects from heavy drinking (especially insomnia) may persist for at least several months, and, before an alcoholic is said to have permanent brain damage, at least a period of that interval should have passed before observations are made. Even then, it may be incorrect to say the alcoholic's impairment came "from" drinking, because the drinking is often accompanied by so many other pathologic influences.

References

1. Time, April 8, 1971

2. Wechsler D: The Measurement and Appraisal of Adult Intelligence (Fourth Edition). Baltimore, Williams & Wilkins, 1958

3. Vaillant GE, Miloffsky ES: Natural history of male alcoholism. Arch Gen Psychiatry 39:127–133, 1982

4. Cox DE, Sipprelle CN: Coercion in participation as a research subject. Am Psychol 26:726–728, 1971

5. White W: Personality and cognitive learning among alcoholics with different intervals of sobriety. Psych Rep 16:1125–1140, 1965

6. Jonsson CO, Croholm B, Izikowitz S: Intellectual changes in alcoholics. Quarterly Journal of Studies on Alcohol 23:221–242, 1962

7. Plumeau F, Marchover S, Puzzo F, et al: Performances of remitted and unremitted alcoholics, and their normal controls. J Consult Psychol 24:240–242, 1960

8. Smith JW, Layden TA: Changes in psychological performance in blood chemistry in alcoholics during and after hospital treatment. Quarterly Journal of Studies on Alcohol 33:379–394, 1972

9. Goldstein G, Chotlos JW, McCarthy RJ, et al: Recovery from gait instability in alcoholics. Quarterly Journal of Studies on Alcohol 29:38–43, 1968

10. Smith JW, Johnson LC, Burdick JA: Sleep, psychological and clinical changes during alcohol withdrawal in NAD-treated alcoholics. Quarterly Journal of Studies on Alcohol 32:982–994, 1971

11. Weingartner H, Faillace LA, Markley HG: Verbal information retention in alcoholics. Quarterly Journal of Studies on Alcohol 32:293–303, 1971

12. Allen RP, Faillace LA, Reynolds DM: Recovery of memory functioning in alcoholics following prolonged alcohol intoxication. J Nerv Ment Dis 153:417–423, 1971

13. Witkin HA, Carp SA, Goodenough DR: Dependence in alcoholics. Quarterly Journal of Studies on Alcohol 20:493–504, 1959

14. Goldstein G, Chotlos JW: Stability of field dependence in chronic alcoholic patients. J Abnorm Psychol 71:420, 1966

15. Carlen PL, Wortzman G, Holgate RC, et al: Reversible cerebral atrophy in recently abstinent chronic alcoholics measured by computed tomography scans. Science 200:1076–1078, 1978

16. Ron MA: The alcoholic brain: CT scan and psychological findings. Psychological Medicine (Suppl. 3). Cambridge, Cambridge University Press, 1983

17. Smith MA, Chick J, Kean DW, et al: Brain water in chronic alcoholic patients measured by magnetic reasonance imaging. Lancet 1:1273–1274, 1985

18. Walker DW, Barnes DE, Zornzetter SF, et al: Neuronal loss in hippocampus induced by prolonged ethanol consumption in rats. Science 209:711–713, 1980

19. McMullen PA, St. Cyr JA, Carlen PL: Morphological alterations in rat CA1 hippocampal pyramidal cell dendrites resulting from chronic ethanol consumption and withdrawal. J Compar Neurol 225:111–118, 1984

20. Kaij L: Alcoholism in twins. Stockholm. Almquist and Wiksell, 1960

21. Drejer K, Theilgaard A, Teasdale TW, et al: A prospective study of young men at high risk for alcoholism: neuropsychological assessment. Alcoholism: Clinical and Experimental Research 9:498–502, 1985

22. Porjesz B, Begletier H: Brain dysfunction and alcohol, in The Pathogenesis of Alcoholism. Edited by Kissin B, Begleiter H. New York, Plenum Press, 1983

23. Schaeffer KWS, Parsons, DA, Yohman JR: Neuropsychological differences between male familial and nonfamilial alcoholics and nonalcoholics. Alcoholism: Clinical and Experimental Research 8:347–351, 1985

24. Reed RJ, Grant I, Adams KM: Family history of alcoholism does not predict neuropsychological performance in alcoholics. Presented at the Ninth Annual International Neuropsychology Society European Conference, Veldhoeven, the Netherlands, June 1986

25. Tarter RE, Hegedus AM, Goldstein G, et al: Adolescent sons of alcoholics: neuropsychological and personality characteristics. Alcoholism: Clinical and Experimental Research 8:216–222, 1984

26. Tewari S, Noble EP: Ethanol and brain protein synthesis. Brain Res 26:469–474, 1971

26. Tewari S, Noble EP: Ethanol and brain protein synthesis. Brain Res 26:469–474, 1971